AMERICAN GARDENS

From
Andy, Ginny, Margi, Bob,
Chicago
U.S.A.

For My 80th Birthday
2022

MONTY DON & DERRY MOORE
AMERICAN GARDENS

PRESTEL

MUNICH · LONDON · NEW YORK

Contents

Previous Monty sitting under a banyan tree.
Opposite The garden at the Sheats-Goldstein House, Los Angeles.   *All captions written by Derry Moore.*

Introduction

This book is both a celebration of a number of beautiful, creative and inspired American gardens, a journey of exploration and, to some extent, discovery.

Despite a long-established partnership that has involved travelling together across the world visiting scores of gardens, Derry Moore and I came to this book from very different positions. Derry first travelled to the USA as a boy and lived there in the 1960s, and since then he has had a close relationship with the country both on a personal and a professional level. Although I have been paying visits since the 1980s, they have been sporadic, tantalisingly brief and always connected with work. I knew enough of the country only to know how little I knew. Whereas Derry had built a network of contacts over many years that enabled us to visit, among others, Bunny Mellon's garden in Virginia and Bob Hope's house in Palm Springs, I knew nobody and had only ever visited two of the gardens before: Monticello and Lotusland. Derry has a unique eye and seeks out beauty wherever he can find it, uninhibited by anything other than the irresistible calling of light and the lens, whereas I come to a garden with all the baggage of history, horticulture and context – not to mention a film crew and a TV series to record.

So from the outset we agreed that we would not be bound to trace each other's footsteps, although by and large they do overlap. We would celebrate our different relationships to and experiences with America and follow them wherever they took us. We mostly travelled together – which is always a joy – although Derry occasionally went off alone and visited gardens that my inevitably tight filming schedule meant I could not get to; and likewise there were some that he had to miss. Occasionally we visited the same place at different times, such as Central Park, which Derry went to in spring to capture its essence as he had got to know it when he lived in New York over fifty years ago, whereas I followed there some months later in a sweltering week in July.

But having visited hundreds of gardens all over the world, I know that no garden stays the same for two days running. There is no perfect moment to visit or absolute season that defines any garden. You dip in, experience it for what it is that day, knowing that the experience carries not just the rest of the year but the whole history of the garden embedded in it, and move on. Tomorrow will be different again. What matters is that you try and capture, be it through the lens of a camera or the pen of a writer, that fleeting, personal impression in order to reach the constant heart of the garden.

The result is not the conventional blow-by-blow account of a series of gardens but two parallel impressions running closely together, based upon a different range of experiences yet with a shared intent that I believe complement and enlarge each other.

For myself, these journeys to different parts of the United States were a quest. I was looking for the American garden. Some garden styles are recognisable and distinctive even if you only have a passing acquaintance with them. Japanese dry gardens, Italian Renaissance gardens, Dutch and French formality, English landscape and cottage gardens, Islamic Charbaghs – all are easily identified and attached to nationalities. But the most common question put to me when setting up this project was 'What *is* an American garden?', as though it were necessary to know the answer in order to justify the trip. So everywhere I went in America I asked people the same question. I never got the same answer twice. Sometimes people simply described the garden they knew best, but more usually they looked puzzled and said that they did not really know. There was a general consensus that the United States is too big and too diverse to possess one characteristic style of garden. What typifies the deserts of Arizona and New Mexico has no relevance in Vermont or Virginia, and the prairies of the Midwest are another horticultural country to Florida.

Opposite The garden at Oak Spring in Upperville, Virginia.

Perhaps that is one of the essences of America. It is an impossibly diverse mixture of climatic zones, landscapes, peoples and cultures that somehow miraculously coheres as a nation. The fact that American gardens resist definition is what makes them particularly American.

When I visited Washington, DC, I had the opportunity to talk to the then British Ambassador, Sir Kim Darroch, about the subject. I wanted to ask him what he thought defined a typically American garden, what I should be looking for, and what influenced Americans' frame of mind when they make and use their gardens. Kim had made it his business to travel as widely as possible across the country during his tenure in Washington, which meant that he had probably seen as wide a variety of its landscapes and its gardens as anyone.

We met in the garden of the British Ambassador's residence on Massachusetts Avenue, with its roses and herbaceous borders and stretch of lawn edged by shrubs – which Kim told me Americans love because they believe it to be quintessentially English. We walked and talked against the backdrop of Edwin Lutyens's vast portico, itself a nod to the Virginia plantation house and in particular Monticello and its four monolithic Ionic limestone columns. Kim told me that American culture has been shaped by the enormity of the continent and its huge amount of open space, of every geographical type, and as a result people seem to want to have their gardens open and unbounded. His lasting impression of America was the variety and sheer vastness of its landscapes. 'And you know, you can't recreate that in the UK, but it imprints itself on your mind. It is something you will keep coming back to.'

The thing that really struck me was Kim's phrase 'you can't recreate that in the UK'. I had seen enough of the country and gazed at every opportunity out of enough windows on internal flights to know exactly what he meant. It is not surprising to discover that America is a big place – a brief scan of a map will tell you that – but until you see it for yourself you have no context with which to measure that bigness. Words to express it fall at the first hurdle. If you have grown up in Britain, or almost anywhere else in Europe, everything – even most mountains, forests and moors – is relatable to a human scale. In Europe a huge landscape can be understood by how small it makes you feel, but in America a huge landscape is just part of a much bigger one. You

disappear into it. Humans cease to be any kind of measure. This makes the landscape an external thing, other and out there, remote and wonderful and mysterious – and ultimately unknowable.

A British garden can brilliantly conjure the essence of a wood or a meadow or even a rocky hillside. But no garden can begin to contain the enormity of the Rockies or the Grand Canyon or the endless expanse of the Midwest. What Kim Darroch seemed to be implying was that the relationship between the natural and domestic worlds, which in British gardens is a linking bridge, is, here in America, a gulf.

Increasingly, Americans leave home in order to connect to the natural world, whereas I think it true to say that increasingly British people find they connect most with the natural world in their gardens. The language that Americans use to describe engagement with nature – 'hiking', 'in nature', 'wilderness', 'trail' – is one that implies adventure and a bracing kind of beauty, and automatically creates a relationship that makes it hard to accommodate into everyday life. 'Growing' in America has immediate connotations of getting bigger, whereas 'growing' in Britain is as much about cultivation and nurturing as expansion. A 'hike' is clearly a step up from and beyond a mere walk, and yet it also a step up and away from the intimacy of the ordinary, everyday perception and interaction that is such an essential feature of gardening. The very best gardens are always personal and essentially domestic, and these are qualities often overwhelmed by the grandeur and sweep of America's astonishing landscape.

James Golden, who knows European gardens very well, has made at Federal Twist, his home in Stockton, New Jersey, what is to my mind one of the great modern gardens. He told me: 'We are still rooted closely into the European garden, but what defines the US garden is an attempt to move away from that and do something different. But it is not a garden culture. Our culture came about through endless expansion through a huge continent. We have not yet learned how to do more with less. We still have the attitude that we can keep expanding.' Of course, there is the archetypal suburban garden, portrayed in a thousand TV series, with the house set back from the road and fronted by an open lawn that runs unbroken down to the pavement and has no barrier with the neighbours. Whole streets are open and dominated by mown

Opposite The swimming pool at the Bob Hope House, Palm Springs.

AMERICAN GARDENS

9

grass. I asked James why this is, given that it is so at odds with the instinctive need of British gardeners to establish boundaries and privacy. He responded: 'At the beginning of the twentieth century there were published, widely disseminated instructions on what a good person would do with his or her house and garden. One thing was a green lawn – which culturally distinguished people from the "dirt poor", where there was literally just dirt and no grass. A lawn instantly showed you to be a cut above that. And putting up a division was considered an act of ill-will towards your neighbours – and indicated you must have something to hide.' These gardens emerged from a very young society still in the process of working itself out, and being seen to have a lawn in front of your house may still today be much more important as a statement of social status than the eccentricity of cultivating a garden. In other words, it is early days. America is still working out what a garden might be and how that relates to the natural world.

And the process is thrilling to observe and enjoy. Derry Moore and I have visited gardens that are the equal of any in the world. All that diversity of people, backgrounds, climates and landscapes is producing an exciting horticultural energy, from street projects in some of the poorest parts of large cities to the vast estates of the very wealthy.

There are many more gardens we should have visited – if only we had more time. But I believe this book is a celebration of the skill, dynamism and sheer optimism of American horticulturalists across the whole nation. If anyone asks 'What *is* an American garden?', direct them to look within these pages.

Above Monty in the garden designed by Steve Martino at Palo Cristi, in Phoenix, Arizona.
Opposite Inside the Amazon Spheres in Seattle.
Overleaf Dumbarton Oaks, Washington, DC.

JOURNEY

ONE

Monticello

Charlottesville, Virginia

While I was in Washington, DC, I went to see the Jefferson Memorial, the monumental figure gazing out between the columns north towards the White House South Lawn in the distance. When Thomas Jefferson moved into the White House in March 1801 it was only just completed, and in 1814, five years after he left it in 1809, the British burnt it to the ground.

Few of the subsequent White House occupants have had Jefferson's wisdom or scholarship; and none his polymathic breadth of interests and knowledge. But then few other humans have. He had an extraordinary mind, voracious, curious, covering every aspect of life from the construction of muskets to the detailed design of buildings, foreign policy, economics and growing perfect peas. We shall return to the peas. His brain was more active than one man could deal with. He was an obsessive recorder of everything – meals, cellars, weather, expenditure, planting, income. As well as being author of the Declaration of Independence, one of the Founding Fathers and serving two terms as president, Jefferson had been minister to France between 1785 and 1789, and in 1786 he crossed the Channel and visited many English gardens. This did nothing to foster a love of the English – he hated them – but this antipathy did not stop him admiring and noting aspects of their gardens, which were to influence his later developments when he returned to America.

Jefferson said that when he was president he thought of his garden every day. When he ceased the presidency, he returned to it and did not leave for the rest of his life. This garden was at Monticello, just outside Charlottesville, Virginia, a hundred miles southwest of Washington, DC. His father had settled there in the 1730s and he inherited the 5,000-acre plantation when he reached 21, in 1764. A few years later, still in his mid-twenties, Jefferson began to build the house, designing every quirky detail, down to the clocks,

dumbwaiters and stair rails, himself. He married in 1772, but his wife, Martha, who bore him six children, died ten years later, before the house was finished. In fact it was never finished to the day he died, 44 years after his wife.

Jefferson's attention to detail and obsession with the place extended outside into the garden. While he was away in Washington he had a large vegetable garden carved out of the hillside to make a 2-acre terrace 1,000 feet long and 90 feet wide. This is held in place on the hillside by a thick retaining wall that took seven enslaved labourers three years to quarry, haul and then build. It was finished in time for his return and soon its 24 squares were filled with over 330 varieties of vegetables, while the orchard below it had 38 varieties of peach, 14 cherry, 12 pear, 27 plum and 24 varieties of grape.

I had visited Monticello in the autumn of 2007, when it was in the grip of a drought; this time, arriving as the sun rose in a fanfare of orange and pink, the garden was green and emerging lushly into spring. The redbud trees were covered in pink blossoms that seemed to bubble up from within the branches. The oaks and limes had that first tentative breaking of leaf that still shows every limb and bough and yet, even on a grey, chilly morning, is effervescent.

Most of the vegetable beds were either empty or planted with as yet young crops, but it was ordered and busy and very well tended. I saw that there were a couple of rows of peas already showing and starting to sprout. Jefferson would have approved. He was clearly obsessed by many things, but none more so, it seems, than the garden pea. He formed the Pea Club with a number of his neighbours, with an annual competition as to who could serve the first dish of fresh peas in the year. In this age of refrigeration and food from every continent and every season available on every street every day of the year, it is worth remembering how limited

Previous The Vizcaya garden, Miami.
Opposite Monticello. The main house was begun in the 1770s; while it was being built, Jefferson and his family occupied a separate pavilion nearby.

the fresh pea season was and how eagerly it must have been anticipated. They were also always a treat, because every pod of peas that was eaten fresh was one pod less to dry and store for winter. It is a measure of the man that although Jefferson won this first pea prize only once, he seemed to derive as much pleasure in others' success as his own.

During his second term as president, Jefferson lobbied hard to stop the importation of slaves, and this resulted in a ban in 1808. The evidence seems to suggest that he hated the concept of enslavement. Nevertheless he kept over four hundred slaves as part of the plantation at Monticello and only freed two in his lifetime. The house, garden and farm were all built and maintained by slaves. This is an uncomfortable, not to say unpalatable, fact that is increasingly hard for modern Americans to reconcile with one of their greatest national figures. I noticed that the difference in the twelve years between my two visits was that while during the former, though ruefully acknowledging this fact, no one really wanted to talk about it; now, people want to talk

about little else. It is as though a stain that was hidden under a carpet has leached out and spread until it is the only thing in the room that people notice. The great vegetable garden with its huge buttressing stone wall has become a symbol of enslavement as much as of horticulture.

The subject remains raw for modern Americans looking back on their great historical leaders – just as it was during Jefferson's time in this part of the South. It has been argued that one of the reasons that Jefferson did not free any slaves was because they represented a financial asset that he needed for collateral. He died in 1826 with huge debts, and Monticello was sold to pay them off. The sale of his slaves helped repay the money that created Monticello. Slavery was always an economic matter as much as a moral one, and few white Americans of the first half of the nineteenth century, slave owners or not, come out of it well. It was complicated and extremely partisan and led, 35 years after Jefferson's death, to a terrible civil war.

Previous The famous vegetable garden created by Jefferson during the years he was president.
Opposite top and bottom The woods at Monticello, with dogwood (*Cornus florida*) and Eastern redbud (*Cercis canadensis*).
Overleaf Flowering dogwood, with the vast horizon of the West stretching out beyond.

Dumbarton Oaks

Washington, DC

Above White wisteria cascades over a garden wall at Dumbarton Oaks.

Above The herbarium border in spring, backed by a box hedge.
Overleaf The pebble garden with the wood beyond, conveying
a sense of the country in the middle of the city.

Previous Climbing fig (*Ficus pumila*) in the orangery at
Dumbarton Oaks.
Above A small, shaded avenue.
Opposite Spring sunlight filtering through the trees in the wood.

British Embassy

Washington, DC

Above The garden with terraces and steps, a typical Lutyens feature.
Opposite Edwin Lutyens's grand portico, with the royal coat of arms, dominates the garden.

Oak Spring

Upperville, Virginia

The plan was to work south from Washington, DC, but first I had the opportunity, through a close connection of Derry's, to visit Oak Spring, the garden of Bunny Mellon, 50 miles west in Upperville.

Bunny Mellon (her real name was Rachel, but her nanny gave her the nickname Bunny and it stuck firmly for the rest of her very long life) was the doyenne of 1960s and '70s gardening in America. She brought to gardens a sense of style and taste that feels comfortably familiar now, but which was new then and became terribly influential. This style was based around a softness and insouciance that was always understated and yet always meticulous and often expensive. The overriding credo was that nothing should be noticed. Everything should appear as though it had just naturally fallen into place – albeit helped by the tight control of a precise and very well-heeled hand. Bunny also introduced the idea of having confidence in the weathering that natural materials acquire though time and use and which adds to their beauty. She gave new money in a young country the confidence to relish the marks of time.

Bunny, herself a considerable heiress, was the wife of Paul Mellon, one of the richest men in the world. Theirs was, by American standards, old money, and with it came a place at the heart of the elite of power and culture. They had houses in Paris, New York, Antigua and Cape Cod, all filled with treasures – particularly a wonderful art collection – of every sort. But her garden at Oak Spring was apparently Bunny's real love. She had no formal training but was a keen gardener from childhood and became, in her day, tremendously influential. She was a style legend. Oak Spring was her base camp, the lodestone of her horticultural style and a particular East Coast sophistication based upon almost limitless wealth.

The first surprise was how relatively modest it is. I had expected a vast mansion and rolling grounds attended by a small army of gardeners, but this is to completely misunderstand Bunny's style. Discretion, ease and artlessness are the watchwords. It is not until you start to add up the details of how it is achieved and maintained that you realise there is a large iceberg of wealth below the surface. The house, through a security gate and down a long drive, is a farmhouse, white with slightly faded (of course) limewash. The yard in front of the entrance has flowers growing through the cracks in the paving, garnered into a soft grid by weathered bricks. The box bushes are trimmed into billowing clouds that spill out from the borders.

Go round the side through a wisteria-draped silvery oak door and you enter into what appears to be a garden within a compound, bounded by a white wall opposite the rear of the house and flanked by smaller stone and white clapboard buildings. These turn out to be guest accommodation; tool sheds; a basket house filled with scores of wicker baskets of every shape and size that were, I was assured, 'just some' of Bunny Mellon's basket collection; and a meeting room approached across a stone-flagged path that spans a pool; all linked on different levels by brick steps and paths in various herringbone and basket weaves. Levels and textures merged and altered but all melded together within the tight parameters of discreet taste.

And flowers. On the April day I was there, the chilly sun shone on beds of tulips in pink, primrose, white and burgundy, and pale lavender phlox and lemon-yellow aquilegias spread beneath the apple trees. Violas bounced and echoed the colours of the tulips, and lily of the valley coyly dipped their bells of white flower among their strappy leaves. Areas of lawn were bounded by step-over apples just budding into blossom. It was charming and fresh and impressive without grandiosity.

Opposite Planting along the path under the archway that leads to the greenhouse.
Overleaf Phlox, aquilegias and violas beneath an apple tree in the spring sunshine.

The main terrace – and there are numerous seating areas within this part of the garden – is paved with stone quarried from the estate. Apparently, two men laboured over this for months, cutting the individual slabs, ferrying them all to the garden and then, with great care and skill, laying them. Bunny Mellon was watching them at work one day and a corner of one of the slabs got broken. The workman lifted the stone and was about to replace it when Bunny stopped him. Leave it, she said, I like it. Then she got a hammer and went round deliberately chipping and breaking others with the precision of an artist with a brush. Into the gaps she had created she sprinkled flower and herb seeds, which quickly grew and spread into the cracks, giving this newly laid terrace a patina of age. This was the epitome of her style, encompassing a certain patrician grandeur and absolute self-confidence with a result that was expensive and meticulous and yet appeared modest and natural.

Go through the double doors at the end of the compound and modesty and naturalness are exchanged for a long pergola made up of a grand avenue of crab apples underplanted with yellow tulips. It leads to a large greenhouse fronted by a pair of swimming pools that, in keeping with the house style, have none of the kitsch garishness of most swimming pools but have the appearance of stylish, stone-edged rectangular basins that you could swim in should you want to.

Bunny Mellon died in 2014 aged 103, a figure from an age that has all but disappeared. Her work and garden, once the very height of fashion, has assumed a historical cast even though it is from a time that I remember well. If this were Britain, Oak Spring would probably have been handed to the National Trust and the story of the Mellons and their money and salacious details would be picked over to become material for a box set. History would gather around it like the flowers creeping out from the gaps in the paving. But the garden is now part of the Oak Spring Garden Foundation, which includes a substantial library and a mission to educate and inform the public on the history and future of plants. This is America, and philanthropy and educational foundations fit easily into the pattern of great wealth; and through it Bunny's work will live on.

In a way this was a twentieth-century diversion visited partly for its convenient location near Washington, and because, through Derry, I could. Oak Spring still feels part of a metropolitan and cultural elite, and through its foundation is connected to and actively fostering the links to the northern centres of power and Europe. But it was now time to enter the true South. This did not involve, in American terms, a long journey, but historically it meant a leap across a huge divide.

Previous A pair of pools divided by a walkway of pleached crab apples.
Opposite top A long pergola of pleached crab apples leads to the orangery.
Opposite bottom The grounds near the house at Oak Spring. Note the dry stone wall.
Overleaf Morning mist at Oak Spring with the traditional split oak fencing in the foreground.
Pages 44–45 Dawn at Oak Spring.

Charleston

South Carolina

Travel invariably involves muddles, cock-ups and silly mistakes. But sometimes it feels as though the fates are amusing themselves by toying with your best-laid plans, and there followed a few days of almost farcical mishaps.

The night before the visit to Monticello, the vehicle taking us and our luggage had broken down, and a replacement took a couple of hours to arrive. Then, an hour before leaving Oak Spring for Charlottesville airport to fly to Charleston, South Carolina, it was pointed out that our tickets were actually from Charlotte, not Charlottesville. For the uninitiated, dropping the 'ville' would have meant an extra 270-mile drive to the airport! However, we managed to get flights from Charlottesville to Atlanta, Georgia – learning along the way that Atlanta's Hartsfield-Jackson airport is the world's busiest – where we changed planes and doglegged east. We landed in Charleston quite a few hours later than planned and with a little more of America visited and not seen, although for an hour or so before dark I sat looking out, reading the landscape from Virginia across North Carolina and into the woods of Georgia that unfolded like a film 30,000 feet below.

Charleston ranks high in polls of 'best places to live' and 'friendliest cities', and it is not hard to see why when you walk the old city centre. The houses in Tradd Street and the French Quarter within the original Charleston city walls are grand, elegant and bigger than they look. They are all built side-on so that their street frontages are the gable ends of long rectangular mansions with gardens beyond. They were built like this so that in the stifling summer heat and humidity – in the days before air conditioning meant everyone sought their shelter from heat behind sealed doors and windows – a breeze could blow right through the length of the house and cool it a little. Verandas run along the length of these sides and much of the summer living, and sleeping, was done in their relative cool. Peeking through the railings and hedges of the street are tantalising glimpses of long, thin gardens with roses and great clumps of amaryllis, and others with salvias growing as great bushes beneath myrtles.

Charleston was one of the most important centres of the slave trade and it has been reckoned that until 1808, when it became illegal, half of all slaves coming from Africa entered America via its port. In the first half of the nineteenth century it was one of the major centres for shipping cotton and built huge wealth – for a tiny minority. It was a city with the highest percentage of black people in America at the time – almost all enslaved – and 4 per cent of the population, based around ninety families, owned and controlled over 80 per cent of its wealth. There was, as Frederick Law Olmsted had reported in the 1850s (before he became a landscape designer), almost no middle class.

The first shots of the Civil War were fired in Charleston when Fort Sumpter was bombarded by South Carolina's militia forces on 12 April 1861 and, after 34 hours, United States Army troops surrendered. The war had begun.

Middleton Place

Follow the Ashley River upstream out of town and it will take you to two plantation gardens, Middleton Place and the Magnolia gardens, both of long-standing fame but very different from each other. In fact, almost all eighteenth- and nineteenth-century visitors coming from Charleston would have come by boat up the river to visit these gardens, as would the plantation owners returning from their grand downtown Charleston houses. We, however, went by road, and on a morning of heavy rain the car radio promised a major storm whipping in from the south. But even driving was a thrill; the road, seen through frantic windscreen

Opposite The pool at Middleton Place, with larger pond beyond.
Overleaf A distinctively Southern style of brick wall at Middleton Place, with enclosed garden beyond.

wipers, was overhung with magnolias and live oaks festooned with Spanish moss. It looked and felt foreign, as far as New York or even Washington feels from London.

Middleton Place is America's oldest landscape garden. Begun in the 1760s by Henry Middleton, a plantation owner who still thought of himself as British, the garden owes much to British as well as French design influences with its mixture of sculpted, flowing parkland and formal symmetry. For nearly ten years an army of enslaved workers dug terraces and carved ponds from the earth. The gardens and the central hall of the house align with a stretch of river so that you look up from the water to the terraced gardens and the house above; and from the house you see the river like a broad canal stretching out as an extension of the wide lawn dividing the two Butterfly Lakes. It is an extraordinary melding of domestic and natural landscape.

The year after Henry's death the French botanist André Michaux introduced evergreen azaleas and camellias to the Southern states. Michaux and Arthur Middleton, Henry's son and heir, became friends, and camellias and azaleas became a vital part of Middleton's planting and the British–French fusion that typifies the garden. But although the horticultural elements of the garden are beautiful, two things stand out above all else. The first is the extraordinary beauty of the trees, and especially the live oaks, *Quercus virginiana*. These are some of the most statuesque and beautiful plants of any kind that I have seen anywhere in the world. The proportion of their breadth in relation to their height, with boughs spreading for nearly 100 feet parallel to the ground that drip with Spanish moss and host long

Above Oak tree branch with the old house beyond.
Opposite An ancient oak tree hung with Spanish moss, suggesting some giant has given it a twist.
Overleaf The oldest live oak tree at Middleton Place.

crests of resurrection ferns, gives them the same grandeur as mountains or a magnificent sea. Their presence gives the sense that the garden is visited by a bigger, wilder nature. The biggest, wildest tree at Middleton Place – and which also claims to be the oldest, if not necessarily the biggest, oak east of the Mississippi – is the Middleton Oak, which is between nine hundred and a thousand years old. It is a vast being, carrying the scars and wounds of a millennium and, despite their famed resilience to storm and fire, lost three huge limbs at the beginning of the twenty-first century. It dwarfs the garden by virtue of its presence and age rather than actual size, seemingly as durable as stone.

Well, not quite. As the weather took a turn for the worse, power failed and roads flooded, so I abandoned my visit. I returned a couple of days later in bright sunshine to find a vast limb, bigger than most oak trees, ripped from the trunk and lying like a collapsed church steeple on the ground. The side branches, still festooned with Spanish moss, now created a thicket of vertical growth. It was like being in the presence of a natural disaster but also a rare, primeval moment. Hundreds of years of growth are shed, smashing the surrounding undergrowth; light pours in; new trees grow. Our presence, the presence of Middleton Place, is of no more consequence than the flight of a passing bird.

The second thing that cannot help but strike any visitor to Middleton Place – or anywhere in the South – follows on from Monticello, and that is the role that slaves played in its creation and management. Slaves were the most essential ingredient in the economy of the South and around Charleston, in particular the economy of growing rice. The extreme wealth of plantation owners like the Middletons depended upon hundreds of enslaved workers. Charles Duell, Henry Middleton's descendant who inherited the estate in 1969, has spent much of his life acknowledging and explaining the role that enslaved workers played at Middleton. He set up the Middleton Place Foundation in 1974, effectively giving the place away so it could be available to the public in perpetuity.

The ruins and rubble of the house are still conspicuously kept as a reminder of the burning of the house by Union soldiers in the Civil War. Just as the wounds of slavery cannot be plastered over and will take time to heal, so too the wounds of the Civil War feel unresolved. It was war fought for financial control more than over slavery, although by the time Middleton Place was razed to the ground in February 1865 the Union was emancipating all slaves. After the war, the South, once so rich, became the poorest part of America, and the resentment remained. This, exemplified in the carefully maintained rubble of the old Middleton Place, is a shocking and heavy burden for a garden to carry. But we are in the South and this is the reality, horticultural as well as political.

Opposite top A live oak tree, the Spanish moss trailing like scarves.
Opposite bottom An alligator rests at the edge of one of the pair of ponds beneath the grassy terraces cut into the hillside.

Magnolia Gardens

A couple of miles down the road – or down the Ashley River – is Magnolia Plantation and Gardens. This may hold the distinction of being the oldest public garden in America. It was certainly public this Easter Saturday, with hundreds of coaches bringing in visitors and children for its annual egg hunt. The gardens get nearly three times as many visitors as their slightly more esteemed neighbour down the road, and I can see why. Middleton Place is grown up and grand and takes its educational and social responsibilities with great seriousness. Magnolia is fun. There is no pressure to absorb or understand its history, although that is there should you wish to inquire into it. The only burden on the visitor is to enjoy the beauty of the place. It is a winning formula and has won out for a long time now.

The house was also burnt down in the Civil War, and its owner, John Drayton, was left almost destitute. He had to sell off much land and property to rebuild it, although the garden was untouched and to help recoup his losses he opened it up five years after the end of the war to trippers coming up the river from Charleston on paddle steamer. Once opened, Magnolia quickly became a major tourist attraction. The 1898 *Baedeker Guide* listed it – along with Niagara Falls and the Grand Canyon – as one of the three places that had to be visited on a trip to the United States.

Whereas Middleton Place remained essentially unchanged until the cataclysm of the Civil War, the key to Magnolia Gardens is that it has embraced change for the past two hundred years. The first garden was a formal, very European affair made in the 1680s adjacent to what was then the house – which burnt down in 1800 and was replaced by one a few hundred yards distant, although remnants of its garden, Flowerdale, remain, laying claim to being one of America's oldest surviving gardens.

John Drayton inherited the 5,000-acre plantation and garden in 1820 and set about changing it away from the French and Dutch formal style to a much looser, British-influenced garden, but – and this is the thing that makes it special – embracing local plants and climate to make something that was uniquely American – a Romantic style of garden. The formality and symmetry typified by Middleton Place was replaced by the use of informal planting designed to inspire an emotional rather than an intellectual response. When camellias began to be introduced in the nineteenth century, Magnolia Gardens embraced and used them enthusiastically – there are now over nine hundred different varieties there – along with azaleas, and these sit easily alongside the native magnolias, oaks and cypresses. There is a maze and a topiary garden and a petting zoo. It has managed to become a theme park and a day out without losing its soul as a garden.

Before leaving Charleston we had our own incendiary incident. We went out to eat and had ordered our food and were discussing the gardens we had seen when suddenly people started screaming, jumping up, knocking over tables and running for the door. I looked up and saw a wall of flame coming from the kitchens. We sat on, being British and not wanting to make a fuss, until we were the only people remaining and a waitress suggested that we were unlikely to receive our food and should probably leave within the next minute or two. As we left, fire engines arrived in force and our dinner, and the restaurant, went up in smoke.

Opposite and overleaf The garden doubled in the water.
Pages 60–61 Foxgloves on the edge of the Ashley River at Magnolia Gardens.

Medway

Charleston, South Carolina

I had long had a romantic idea of Medway, which I had heard much about but never visited, and was thrilled when the present owner allowed me to photograph there. The previous owner, Mrs Gertrude Legendre, who bought the place in 1930 and died in 2000, made the huge property into a trust to preserve wildlife, thereby protecting it from the encroachment of housing developers. It didn't disappoint, being every bit as romantic as I had imagined. – DM

Opposite Looking through an archway into the walled garden.
Above A curved wall sits behind clipped box hedges.
Overleaf The house and live oak trees beyond the walled garden.

Above Looking through Spanish moss-covered branches to the stable building.

Above Oak tree branches overhanging the edge of the lake.
Spanish moss festoons all the branches of the great oaks at Medway.

Vizcaya

Miami, Florida

Everybody is a sucker for the sun, and Florida has almost endless sun without ever being too hot or too humid. No wonder it has been the place where people holiday or retire to, buying or building themselves a home under this benign sun. But few have done so with the panache, not to say eccentricity, of James Deering – and in Miami that is really saying something.

William Deering, James's father, had made money providing the Union Army with uniforms in the Civil War and then used the profits to invest in developing the Deering harvester machine. Having spent years of my life making, lifting, stacking and then using bales of hay and straw, this strikes a particularly personal note. The key to this harvester was that it not only cut the crop much faster and more efficiently, therefore hugely increasing the profits for Midwest farmers, but also bound it in twine – which Deering manufactured and sold too. It immediately made huge profits. In 1902 Deering's company merged with two others to form the International Harvester Company, which became the largest producer of agricultural machinery in the nation and whose tractors can still be seen cultivating fields around the world – including from the room in which I write these words.

James Deering was 43 when this merger made him limitlessly rich. He already owned houses in Chicago, New York and Paris but he developed pernicious anaemia and was advised to spend his winters away from the cold of Chicago, so he went south and in 1912 bought 180 acres of land in the Biscayne area of Miami, near an estate his brother already owned. On this land he built his house and garden, which he called Vizcaya.

Everything about Vizcaya is operatic, staged and mannered – and none the worse for that. It is house and garden as performance in the same vein as Isola Bella, or indeed any of the great Italian houses and gardens from which it derives so much. Guests would arrive by boat into a little harbour created by a breakwater modelled to look like a barge, and then, guided by the striped Venetian landing posts, take the steps up onto the quay or terrace and on up into the house, built to look like a Tuscan palazzo. Deering had travelled extensively in Italy and cherry-picked ideas, designs and actual objects – even whole rooms – to assemble a kind of Renaissance and Baroque greatest hits; a sixteenth- and seventeenth-century medley played out under the Florida sun.

To do so involved extraordinary feats of skill, engineering, stubbornness and expense. A thousand people worked on the estate between 1914 and 1923, although Deering spent his first Christmas there in 1916. The site was essentially a mangrove swamp and wholly unsuited to a building of any kind – let alone one like this. It is the very model of what optimism and shameless borrowing from another culture can achieve given limitless money from technological and industrial development.

As well as the house and gardens Deering built a compound to house his staff and provide them with communal recreation rooms, workshops, a small farm and a large vegetable garden, all part of a self-sustaining estate. The gardens, which are beautifully made and beautifully restored and maintained despite hurricanes and the depredations of time, blithely cherry-pick aspects from Italian gardens. There are pools, cascades and fountains, a grotto, topiary, clipped lines of trees and parterres, a theatre garden and maze garden, a casino raised on a mound, and glorious flights of steps balustraded and bedecked with urns. Some of this was shipped over from Italy, such as the fountain from Sutri, near Villa Lante and the Palazzo Farnese, which Deering visited along with his designer Paul Chalfin; some items were modified and some invented.

Opposite Italian Baroque at its most fanciful and exuberant in one of the many enclosed areas at Vizcaya.
Overleaf The house reflected in a pool – one of many places revealing the influence of Tuscan villas.

In this Italian fantasy, live oaks, palms, orchids and bromeliads happily, and surreally, grow. It is a full-blown tropical Italianate Renaissance garden.

To somehow create this fantasy in a mangrove swamp in a place 1,500 miles from its spiritual home was an act of extreme escapism, making a garden as unconnected to both Deering's own life and the place as possible. It sets Deering, the slightly remote, wealthy bachelor inviting the rich and famous to play in this fantasy land in the sun by the sea, as a Gatsbyesque figure, always slightly apart. In fact he seems to have had a real interest in the local ecology, and one of the reasons that he built the house in such an unpromising position – rather than a little higher up on the rocky outcrop where he built the casino – is that he wished to preserve the local stone and its flora rather than aggressively cut into it. In Deering's time the mangrove swamp and native forest stretched out all around, hiding all but the sea. Now downtown Miami can be seen dominating the view as you look out east, its skyscrapers bouncing light between the blue of sky and sea. There are those that see this as a desecration, vandalising the magic of the place, but I rather like it. It just adds another layer of surrealism to a place that turns reality on its head.

Deering died in 1925, returning from a trip to Europe. Vizcaya went to his nieces, who sold off much of the estate piecemeal and then in 1952 the residue to Miami-Dade County as a museum.

Above Columns and obelisks dotted around the garden enhance the atmosphere of sixteenth- and early seventeenth-century Italy.
Opposite Staircase reflected in a pool. The entrance to the grotto can be glimpsed on the right. As with everywhere in Vizcaya, the features have a fullness of scale that reflects a deep understanding of Italian sixteenth-century gardens – perhaps eclectic, but not pastiche.
Overleaf Not Venice but a man-made island designed to resemble a barge, with the coloured poles of the Venetian canals. The modern world (Miami) can be glimpsed in the distance.

Vizcaya is a potent emblem of what America did and does better than any culture since the court of Louis XIV, which is to create a garden as a wholly artificial dominion, shaping, controlling and conquering the landscape in order to make a stage on which humans can play and admire. To some extent all gardens have always done this, but rarely to such a degree. It is a symbol of the extreme wealth that technology and farming was creating, and at the same time a profound disconnect from the natural world – which America had in more abundance and splendour than anywhere else on earth – and the domestic landscapes that were being created.

I went from Vizcaya to Miami Beach and walked on the broad stretch of sand, backed by a fringe of palm trees below the stacks of apartment blocks on one side and a strip of azure sea beneath an enormous pale blue sky on the other. Hundreds soaked up the last of the evening sun, played and displayed their tans. This was the natural world that they liked best and felt most comfortable with. It is a long way from a garden.

Opposite Monty in the garden at Vizcaya.
Above A reflection of Miami.
Overleaf Selfie heaven in downtown Miami.

Longue Vue

New Orleans, Louisiana

Herbie, our wonderful guide at Magnolia Gardens in Charleston, had corrected me sharply when I said that I was going to visit 'New Orleans'. 'You say it like that an' they're going to *laugh* at you boy. It ain't *New Orleens* but *Norlins*. It's Norlins.'

From that moment, every time I started to say 'New Orleans' I had a fit of self-conscious mispronunciation and ended up mangling it horribly. But New Orleans is a jumble of cultures, with Cajun, Creole, African American and French, among others, so there is probably some poetic justice in that. It seemed amazing that Jefferson had bought it from Napoleon for $15 million – along with 828,000 square miles of land west of the Mississippi, reaching from New Orleans into what is now modern Canada, doubling the size of the United States in the process. Most of this was occupied for millennia by Native Americans, who, of course, were never consulted or included in any way in the deal.

Norlins is a city of gardens, and I spent a happy day wandering around the French Quarter, with its wrought-iron balustrades and painted shutters, and the Garden District, where the streets were heavy with the fragrance of star jasmine and the magnolias were beginning to flower, trying Southern food and visiting Congo Square in Louis Armstrong Park, where Catholic slaves would gather on a Sunday to dance and drum out their rhythms, drawing together their traditions and forging the music that was to evolve into jazz.

It is the random, happened-upon details that build our imagined cultures. I had built a Southern world based almost entirely on books and films and, as much as anything else, on the strangeness of the food. Grits summoned to my mind texture rather than taste; gumbo felt like it could apply to a musical style as much as a dish; and although there were biscuits and gravy aplenty in my world, they never appeared together on the same plate and rarely in the same meal. So the real culture shock in arriving in New Orleans was to discover that my imagination was wildly astray. Grits turned out to be a kind of loose polenta; biscuits were not crisp and biscuity at all but doughy – effectively scones; and gravy a rather runny white sauce. Gumbo came to the rescue in its assorted forms, all delicious, fulfilling all my preconceptions as a fish stew.

I didn't feel disappointed with any of this so much as off beam. It was as though I had found that the place I was steadfastly aiming for was in fact miles away from my destination. So I had to stop assuming and start to pay attention to what was actually there. It is as good an attitude as any to adopt when you visit a garden for the first time.

Everybody has an angle. There are those who seek out unusual plants; others who try to find the bit that they would like to have outside their own house. When I visit a garden I try not to let anything that I know about it come to the fore, at least for the first half-hour or so, and give first impressions a chance to be just that. I never know what I am looking for but am pretty sure that I will recognise it when I see it. It might be a shady corner, a view, a particular grouping of plants or the sense of place that defines a garden – the hub from which all the rest spins out. Then I start to piece together the evidence before my eyes with the available facts, and inevitably that colours my feelings or interpretation of what I have seen. So I take a second look, marry these things together and see where that takes me. There are times when none of this happens and I am left untouched – when nothing is happening and the garden and I become less than the sum of our parts. But this is rare and probably down to tiredness or ignorance.

All this was running through my mind as I started to walk around Longue Vue gardens. The front has a grand avenue of live oaks leading to an impressively grand facade, but the back of the house is more of a piece with a columned portico overlooking a long lawn flanked by flower-filled parterres that arrives at a canal whose arcing jets of water along either side

Opposite The avenue of live oaks leading to the house at Longue Vue.

clearly derive from the Generalife gardens at the Alhambra in Spain. It is stately, even magisterial, and conjures a pre-Civil War plantation house and estate. But though this impression might be meaningful, the facts are very different.

Edgar Stern and Edith Rosenwald married in 1921 and built their first house at Longue Vue, in the Metairie suburb of New Orleans, in 1925 on a modest plot next to the local golf course, although because they were Jewish they were not allowed to join. Both were wealthy, Edith from the fortune that her father made with Sears, Roebuck & Co.; and Edgar, whose family emigrated from Germany to New Orleans at the end of the nineteenth century, from his own business in the cotton trade. They gradually bought more land and made a garden, but it was not until their return from a trip to Europe in 1936, when they were inspired by visits to many gardens, that the Longue Vue that you now see came into being.

They hired the garden designer Ellen Biddle Shipman, who was a pioneering feminist in what was then very much a male-dominated gardening world. Working with Edith Stern, Shipman laid out an extensive and dramatic series of gardens. Most gardens, big or small, are made around an existing house and work off it, but at Longue Vue the new garden had taken on a life of its own and was overwhelming the building. So the Sterns, unabashed, built a new house on a new site, bigger, grander and with a different facade on each of the four sides that would now relate directly to the garden, which had trebled in size from the original plot and extended to over 8 acres with fourteen different compartments or separate gardens. And in what seems to me a very American detail, the original house was winched and dragged to a new site further down the road. Because they could.

Above The side of the house overlooking the Spanish Courtyard.
Opposite The dappled shade on the grass from the avenue of overhanging live oaks.
Overleaf Entrance to the house seen through the trees.

The new house had garden vistas on three sides, although the fourth looks directly over the golf course. It says much both about the Sterns' lack of bitterness and the American desire to literally be seen to be above board that there was no attempt to screen off the golf course, either to hide the ambling Gentile golfers in their dreadful golfing clothes or to stop the members gawping in at the Sterns' new garden.

The initial planting of the garden was based upon European gardens and particularly on Spain, but Edith Stern was interested in the local Louisiana wildflowers and wanted to champion them. Gradually the garden went from a crafted pastiche of a European garden to one that sat firmly in its Louisiana context, full of plants that thrived locally – which was just as well, because many of the Mediterranean plants found the southern summers too humid.

The garden has also had to deal with southern storms. Hurricane Betsy in 1965 was followed by substantial remodelling; and as well as blowing down over two hundred trees, Hurricane Katrina in 2005 left the garden under nearly 2 feet of water for two weeks, which killed around 60 per cent of all the plants in the garden – although all the live oaks survived despite completely defoliating for a year. It took work by over six hundred volunteers for the first year to clear the mess and repair the damage, and another seven years for the garden to get back to where it had been.

Climate change in this part of the world means that further huge storms are almost inevitable, although in the scheme of things damage to a garden is the least of anyone's problems. To put that into context, after Hurricane Katrina, five out of the six full-time gardeners never returned to the garden because 85 per cent of all local housing stock had been destroyed. With nowhere to live they simply left.

I went back into the centre of New Orleans and down to the banks of the Mississippi, where college students lolled on the mown grass and played frisbee and threw footballs around barbecues, young, bright and optimistic. The vast barges slowly headed from the port upstream against a strong current, with the grinding and screech of a goods train half a mile long in the background. The energy and sheer volume of the water flowing from Minnesota over 2,000 miles down here to the Mississippi Delta, and all that country aside it, seemed unimaginably, dizzily vast. I was reminded of Ambassador Darroch's words to me about his abiding impression of America's vast landscape: 'you can't recreate that in the UK, but it imprints itself on your mind. It is something you will keep coming back to.' Gardens, especially the average, modest suburban garden, can seem trivial, even irrelevant, in the face of this. But I was beginning to realise that it is also the key that unlocks the door to understanding what defines American gardens and gives them an identity.

Opposite top Looking from the house across the parterre.
Opposite bottom At the side of the garden, with lawn and box-enclosed beds.
Overleaf The great Mississippi River.

JOURNEY

TWO

Lurie Garden

Chicago, Illinois

It is a strange thing to fly halfway across the world to one of the most famous cities on the planet, and one that you have never visited, and then to stay for less than 24 hours in order that you might see a single garden – and practically nothing else other than the road from the airport. The object of this fleeting visit to Chicago was the Lurie Garden, 2.5 acres of intense planting. Despite being at ground level it is in fact a roof garden, as the entire thing is built on top of a car park dug into what had been an abandoned railway siding in the centre of the city. It is part of the larger Millennium Park, situated in the Loop, the city's business district.

I like the story of the genesis of this park. Until the mid-1990s the rights to the area were owned by Illinois Central Railroad, and it consisted of railway tracks and wagons, just as it had done since the 1850s. Apparently the then mayor, Richard M. Daley, would look down on this semi-abandoned railway site, by then partially used as a parking lot, when visiting his dentist. Either his teeth needed a lot of work or he was scrupulously regular with his dental check-ups, but he saw it often enough for it to bother him, and he decided to do something about it. In 1997 he persuaded the Illinois Central Railroad to donate the land back to the city. The transformation began. The architect Frank Gehry designed a concert pavilion for the project, while the sculptor Anish Kapoor created a reflective, billowing sculpture titled *Cloud Gate*, known universally as The Bean.

Millennium Park officially opened in 2004, with a portion of its 24 acres devoted to the Lurie Garden. However, you could visit one without being aware of the other, and in fact the wall of buildings rising into the Chicago sky (a brilliant blue the day I was there) seems a more apt backdrop than the rest of the park on the other side.

The design of the garden was put out to competition, and it was won by the combination of the landscape architecture firm Gustafson Guthrie Nichol and the Dutch plantsman Piet Oudolf. In fact the garden, because of its distinctive planting style, is often referred to as Oudolf's, but the layout, with its high flanking hedges and sweeping central wooden path that bisects the two parts of the garden, one open and the other shaded by a grove of trees, is a superb combination of landscaping and plant design. The wooden boardwalk with a stream running beneath it is a nod towards the miles of boards placed down on the muddy ashen ground after the terrible Chicago fire of October 1870 that destroyed around 17,000 buildings and over 2,000 acres of the city. The limestone edging to the borders, with its monumental scale and rough-hewn surfaces, looks and feels like remnants from a large building. The lines are clean and strong and provide the perfect setting for the planting.

And the planting is stunning. I have seen gardens by Piet Oudolf all over Europe but this stands supreme both in detail and setting. It is a masterpiece. Oudolf has become a guru for the age of 'New Perennial' and grass planting, where great tufts of grasses and herbaceous perennials in large, mainly informal borders replicate the openness of the prairie and yet have the subtlety and finesse of the garden. He is now rightly revered across the world, but for many years he was primarily a nurseryman based at Hummelo in the Netherlands. The Lurie Garden was his first public competition and his first garden in America. I cannot believe that it will ever be bettered. This is because the setting is so monstrously beautiful, with skyscrapers pilastering the sky above the metallic curves of Gehry's music hall, shining like samurai armour, and the curving lines of the immense surrounding hedge of beech, hornbeam and thuja holding the garden in from this overwhelming cityscape. It is a garden that is improved by the incongruity of its setting.

We went at dawn, long awake (jet lag leaves one fuddled with tiredness at hopeless times of day but also brings an

Opposite The Lurie Garden, showing the contrast between the 'wild' meadow and the glass and steel city behind.

alertness to other parts of the day and night that are not normally reached), to see the sun filtering through the trees on the eastern side of the garden and delicately touching the backs of the coneflowers as well as casting great blocks of shadow. The scale of the planting holds its own against the grandeur and drama of this backdrop with huge drifts of pink echinacea, *Salvia nemorosa*, elecampane, stachys and the common milkweed jewelled with monarch butterflies like flying stained-glass windows, feeding up on nectar before their impossibly long journey south. Oudolf has become associated with the extensive use of grasses, often executed as a kind of tall, not very flowery meadow, but grasses do not dominate here at all and the garden in midsummer was garlanded with swathes of colour and light.

It grew hot and busy. As the working day began, more and more people walked through, clearly taking great pleasure from the garden's existence. In fact, over twenty

million people a year visit Millennium Park. Laura Ekasetya, the Lurie's head gardener (or, as Americans prefer, Director and Head Horticulturist), told me that one of the biggest problems that they have to deal with is the damage caused by people taking selfies, as visitors back into the borders to get a better shot. I have heard a litany of problems from gardeners all over the world but this was the first time that I had come across that particular horticultural difficulty.

Time to go and see another, much more rural, version of the prairie. Was it worth going all the way to Chicago just to see one garden and practically nothing else at all? Of course it was.

Above Anish Kapoor's *Cloud Gate* in Millennium Park, adjoining the Lurie Garden.
Opposite Frank Gehry's open-air concert hall in Millennium Park with its dramatic sculptural effect. The light catches so beautifully on the metal, adding to the drama.
Overleaf The Lurie Garden, looking towards the Modern Wing of the Art Institute of Chicago and late nineteenth-century buildings behind.

Prairie Garden Trust

New Bloomfield, Missouri

Arriving at Columbia Regional Airport in Missouri is like landing in Stornoway in the Outer Hebrides – or at least the Stornaway I last flew into twenty-odd years ago. You amble off the plane into a low, single-storey hut where 'Its a Long Way to Tipperary' plays on what sounds like a xylophone as the single luggage carousel slides out of the wooden wall. The contrast to Chicago is staggering, refreshing and above all a measure of how big America is – after a short flight that barely marks the map, you are in every way miles away.

Early the next morning, having eventually found our hotel despite going in the opposite direction for over an hour, we set off for the Prairie Garden Trust. This is not so much a garden as an idea. It is a showcase and a sanctuary for the landscape that was here before industrial farming pillaged it. The husband-and-wife team of Henry and Lorna Domke run and maintain the trust as a kind of educational example of what can be done to land that has been conventionally farmed. The garden has no function other than to inspire. You cannot hire it for weddings, and the Domkes do not aspire to serious research. It just is; and that – spendidly, spectacularly – is enough.

The story began in 1971 when Henry's parents, Herb and Joan Domke, moved to Jefferson City. Herb was a hospital administrator and wanted to live in the countryside rather than the city. Rural land was cheap, so they bought 80 acres of it. This has expanded to over 500 acres, of which 300 are glorious woods heading out to the Ozarks. The rest is prairie – not with the vast horizons of the tall-grass prairie that I had visited a decade ago near Cotton Falls in Kansas, but that liminal area where the woodlands of the east meet the open prairies of the Midwest, combining the best of both. The trees depended upon a rainfall – about 40 inches a year – that was twice that of the open prairies further west, so the horizon was edged in every direction by woodland, with

the prairies like huge fields rather than the rolling expanses where vast herds of buffalo roamed before they were systematically exterminated.

But this contained, cultured prairie was hard won. Herb had nurtured the woods and built ponds but the grassland remained obdurately resistant to naturalisation, the fescue bred and sown by previous farmers dominating all the natural grasses and flowers. They tried every kind of organic approach to removing it, without success, and so finally resorted to spraying it with glyphosate and then reseeding with indigenous grasses along with all the native Missouri flowers that inspired the Lurie and so many other subsequent prairie gardens.

Herb died in 1991, and Henry, who was a GP for many years before retiring to work full time at the trust, took on the project. He and Joan live modestly but exude a calm satisfaction at the life they have made, based as it is around constant hard work. The two of them, both in their mid-sixties, look after the 540 acres with the help of only two other workers. In February 2004 a fire burnt down the farmhouse and it has now been replaced by a visitor centre where groups can come to be educated, informed and inspired by this vision of their prairie birthright.

I am very familiar with an English hay meadow, filled with flowers in the few months before harvest and then grazed tight for half the year, the grass deliberately low and sparse so the flowers can compete. But this was the concept of a meadow taken to another dimension. Coneflowers, liatris, monarda, phlox and wild indigo grow by the tens of thousands. You do not walk so much as wade chest- or even head-high through the flowers. Birds – over 150 different species – and butterflies love it. British meadows are billowing, soft places, but under the heat of the Midwestern

Opposite The Prairie Garden project is situated exactly at the point where the open prairies of the Midwest meet the heavily wooded landscape of the east. This field of coneflowers with trees and cloud-filled sky behind conveys a sense of the vastness of the Midwest.

summer sun the harsh rigidity of the flower stalks and the sharp edges of the grasses made this a harder, much more dramatic scene. And unlike the European meadow this is not harvested annually for hay but instead, every three years, rotating the fields, the Domkes burn and then reseed it in a dramatic act of renewal. For all its beauty and environmental boldness, this is a floral frontier that is not for the faint-hearted.

But that is the point. Henry and Joan Domke, respectable, educated, liberal, generous and wise, are tough too. What they are creating is difficult and way out of the comfort zone of their farming neighbours. This is an America taken to a place it barely recognises as its own, despite the fairly recent historic precedent. It walks the boundary between the domestic and the romanticised versions of nature that modern America places on a pedestal but rarely integrates into daily life. Unlike the tightly mown lawns running down to the street or the monoculture of fields, this is nature that is not wild or remote or dramatically other, but fecund and diverse and complicated as well being accessible and almost domestic.

As well as beautiful, it is brave.

Opposite Thistles in the Prairie Garden.
Above The lush garden encourages an array of wildlife to gather, including butterflies and other insects.
Overleaf The road leading to the property, banked with flowers and with a well-used mailbox – a frequent sight at the entrance of American properties – with signal flag.

Central Park

Manhattan, New York City

On a hot July day, walking a mile of Fifth Avenue uptown from 59th Street to the Met (worth the walk, the queue and the crowd – worth the flight, dammit – just to see a single Rembrandt self-portrait), the trees of Central Park line the road with a deep, shady seduction. On the way back, heady with wonderful paintings, I dip gratefully into its embrace.

Central Park used to be such a scary place. During the day, dealers, muggers and worse lurked in the bushes, and darkness brought demons. That was in the 1970s and '80s, but now it is safe, inviting and arguably more beautiful than it has ever been. The trees have reached their maturity without suffering from age and it is carefully looked after without being fussily primped. All of it is now accessible and no other park has such a variety of landscape, from the open lawns of the Sheep Meadow to the wooded area of the Ramble and the formality of the English Garden. By and large, inside this rigidly gridded, manic city it seems a natural piece of landscape unspoilt by man.

Nothing, of course, could be further from the truth. Apart from the larger stone deposits, almost every single aspect of the 843-acre park is artfully constructed. Every undulating tree, pond and most of the rocks were planned and placed. That this was done, in collaboration with the architect Calvert Vaux, by a journalist and author, Frederick Law Olmsted, seems astonishing. Prior to entering the competition for Central Park in 1858, Olmsted, who was a farmer as well as a journalist, had never drawn, designed or made any kind of landscape. Had he never entered the field of landscape design he still would have been an important figure, however. At a time when cotton was a vital commodity with huge trade both within America and across the Atlantic, and the association with slavery tolerated for the riches it created, his extensive reporting in the mid-1850s from the South for the *New York Daily Times* exposed the underlying fragility and hollowness of the Southern slave economy and the Southern social structure.

But Central Park not only eclipsed Olmsted's other work but went on to be the precursor for Chicago's Riverside Park, Prospect Park in Brooklyn and other parks around the United States, as well as university campuses and housing projects. Throughout the Civil War he worked for the Sanitary Commission tending the wounded and sick, and he was also an early conservation campaigner. In all, he was a toweringly influential figure in shaping both the way that urban America looks and the way it thinks about landscape and its relationship with the natural world. Whereas the parks that Olmsted saw in Britain were based on the landscape gardens of grand houses, Olmsted designed public spaces as versions of the grandeur of the American landscape, which was still largely untamed and unspoilt.

The whole concept of a park as a public space was a new one both in Britain and the US; the first British park, Derby Arboretum, had only opened in 1840. Olmsted visited England in 1850, where he visited Derby along with the other parks that were increasingly being made in a wave of educational philanthropism. It was a very Victorian concept and meant that these first nineteenth-century public parks were intended as places where workers could enjoy fresh air and exercise for their physical and moral well-being as well as leisure. One of the parks Olmsted visited was Birkenhead Park, not far from where his boat docked at Liverpool. Birkenhead was the first park to be created in Britain with public money and was designed in 1847 by Joseph Paxton, who at the time of Olmsted's trip was still head gardener at Chatsworth House but at the height of his fame and working on the Crystal Palace for the Great Exhibition of 1851. Olmsted saw in Birkenhead a democratic ideal and wrote, 'I was ready to admit that in democratic

Opposite Bloomsbury in Central Park.
Overleaf The trees in Central Park were planted in the mid- to late nineteenth century and are now reaching maturity.

America there was nothing to be thought of as comparable with this People's Garden.'

On his return, Olmsted insisted from the outset that Central Park should be open and equally accessible to all the inhabitants of the city. It certainly seems that way from the picnickers, readers, ball players, skateboarders, dog walkers, buskers mangling Beatles songs at Strawberry Fields, boaters on the lake and cyclists swishing between the best-dressed guests bossily marshalled by wedding planners. It is New York balancing itself, finding the yin to the yang of the remorseless, thrilling streets.

As Central Park neared completion Olmsted visited Britain again, and this trip reinforced his leaning towards a naturalistic design along the lines of the English landscape movement rather than the much more formal layouts of Continental grand estates. Above all it confirmed his goal of creating in Central Park a real sense of being immediately in countryside, surrounded by one of the busiest cities in the world.

But although there are these British influences, Central Park neither looks nor feels like any British counterpart. Its size, the use of giant rocks, the variety of landscapes and the sense of exploration that residents still talk about after years of living in the city make it both unique and also particularly American.

Above The statue on the Bethesda Fountain was designed in 1868 by Emma Stebbins, the first woman sculptor to receive a public commission in New York.
Opposite The lake, overlooked by the two towers of the San Remo apartment building, designed by Emery Roth in 1930.
Overleaf A couple enjoying the evening peace, seated on one of the giant rocks that are such a feature of Central Park.

Eagle Street Rooftop Farm

Brooklyn, New York City

When I first visited New York back in the early 1980s we would eat in diners that fulfilled every expectation and matched every image that we had seen on screen. Hash browns, eggs over easy, crispy Canadian bacon, pancakes, toast, orange juice and unlimited coffee, all ladled out with extravagant abundance. But now the traditional diner is a rarity. However, we found one in Queens and breakfasted well before visiting the Eagle Street Rooftop Farm in the Greenpoint neighbourhood of Brooklyn. It is certainly on Eagle Street, and it is up on a roof, but 'farm' overplays the hand a little. Nevertheless, the serried rows of raised beds filled with vegetables and herbs set against the stunning views across the East River to the Lower East Side are an extraordinary sight.

The farm sees itself as a model for a sustainable urban future. The produce from its 6,000 square feet (just over a tenth of an acre, or two traditional allotment plots) supplies a weekly Saturday market as well as up to ten local restaurants through the season. One of the people working there told me that there are potentially 3,000 acres of serviceable roof space like this in New York that could be used to grow vegetables. This means that if they were all used, New York City could be self-sustaining in fresh, seasonal organic herbs and vegetables.

The technical problems of growing good vegetables on a roof centre mostly around the need for extra-sharp drainage so that weight does not build up, and exposure to both wind and hot sun which means that the beds dry out fast and need very regular watering. In practice, the shallow beds and exposed position of Eagle Street mean that Mediterranean herbs and plants such as chillies thrive best, whereas the more water-dependent vegetables struggle. However, the roof is designed to retain an inch and a half of rain, which as well as acting as a reservoir for the plants also cools the building and saves on air-conditioning costs. They make their own compost but buy in, rather exotically, bat guano as a supplementary fertiliser.

To reach the farm I had to go up in a lift and then down a corridor, walk up some stairs and through a door to cross a roof, and then up another set of rickety stairs. Getting all the materials up there must have been a caper. But this is New York, where towering buildings, gardens in the sky and rooftop farms are all handled with panache and aplomb. One hundred tons of special growing medium, made from compost, rock dust and shale, were craned onto the roof during the course of a single day in 2010. But everything else, from the volunteers to the produce, has to come down exactly the way that I came up.

All the workers are young, enthusiastic and extremely environmentally concerned. Their work on the roof is as much a form of activism as it is horticulture. Sarah Bos, a 25-year-old food writer who works there part time as part of her process of learning about food, talked to me as she weeded a bed of basil. She told me that the team all see this as a strike against mass-produced food and the poor human and animal welfare that has resulted from the pursuit of profit rather than health and well-being, and that there is a growing sense of this among their friends and contemporaries. Alice works there three days a week and is happy to make the two- hour journey each way from Staten Island, not just for the good that she believes the garden is achieving for the community but for the good it is doing her. However unusual or even unlikely the location, working the soil and nurturing plants is working the same healing magic on her as it does on so many of us all across the world. To have this available in the innermost part of the innermost of all cities, working for individuals and the community at large, seems profoundly important.

There is an evangelical, bright-eyed quality to the Eagle Street farm that might make a world-weary cynic's eyebrow lift a little, and the quality of the produce is variable compared to that grown in the rich loam of a well-tended English allotment – but that is to miss the point. This is brave and pioneering and feels like a new frontier.

Target Bronx Community Garden

The Bronx, New York City

Patches of garden, parkland and parking lots have gradually been swallowed up across New York, as in every other city across the world, by housing developments. Developers being what they are, these invariably are high-end apartments and do nothing to alleviate housing problems for those who need it most. Thus gentrification gradually spreads until an area becomes fashionable and expensive and the poor and their families and established communities are edged further out. It happens everywhere. But the combination of the active engagement of the actress Bette Midler and the support and finance of the city's former mayor, billionaire Michael Bloomberg, has done something remarkable to strike against this – with gardens.

The New York Restoration Project has set up 52 gardens across five boroughs in the the city, all of them rescued from the developers' bulldozers. I went to The Bronx, bowling up Park Avenue early on a Saturday morning when only joggers and dog walkers collecting bags of breakfast bagels were about. On Anderson Avenue, within the shadow of Yankee Stadium, is the Target Bronx Community Garden. There is nothing to see from the street other than a wooded bank behind railings and in one corner a steep path dipping under a yew tree hung with signs saying 'Welcome', 'Relax' and 'Smile'.

At the top of the path was a bright, open space half-filled with sixteen raised beds, all full of a wide variety of vegetables, herbs and fruit; a big lawn that was being used by about thirty women for a yoga class; at one end an open-fronted building with a long table; and at the other end of the site a little library with child-sized seats, a loo and a tool shed. A large outdoor kitchen, shaded by a peach tree hung with fruit, held the centre ground.

This space was felt good and busy with chatter, most of it funny, rude and wise. Although the atmosphere was kind and welcoming, the edges were sharp and irreverent. The beds were often shared and some were weedy, some scant and tentative,

but others packed with vegetables expertly grown. On this Saturday morning there were young children helping out, weeding, harvesting. There were a lot of tomatoes, herbs and, somewhat surprisingly, spring greens. Miriam Tab, the coordinator and liaison officer for the site, told me that she really liked collards – American English for spring greens – and that she cooked them with some pork or bacon for real Southern flavour. She was also harvesting tomatoes, but green, because 'fried green tomatoes are the best'. A young couple, he with an armful of tattoos and she with various studs and spikes adorning her face, were gently showing their young son their plot and selecting a few chillies, carrots and tomatoes for their dinner. The child eyed me suspiciously over the top of a freshly pulled carrot that he was chewing. They said that they lived in an apartment nearby and could 'look out on our garden' from their bathroom window. Another woman, impossibly young-looking but with three children, was gathering peaches from the tree. I helped reach some higher up. She said she was going to make a pastry with them. What sort, I asked. 'Just a puff pastry with peaches and honey and nutmeg and cinnamon. You bake it briefly. Then I make homemade coconut ice cream and serve it with that.' For all her youth and modest manner, the 'bake it briefly' betrayed her. I asked what she did. 'I'm a chef. But I like to grow as much as I can. It's not just for the good things, but so I know about them too.' Would that all chefs were this wise.

I have visited many community gardens and projects that have a slightly uncomfortable air of self-congratulation. They are doing good and they know it. The Target Bronx Community Garden has not a whiff of that. They are not so much doing good as being good.

Madoo Conservancy

Sagaponack, New York

I went to Long Island to visit a couple of gardens in the Hamptons. As you leave Queens and head out into Long Island along the Northern State Parkway with its low bridges and retro charm, Long Island becomes a holiday resort. It takes New York out to the ocean and does so via some of the most spectacular beaches in the whole of the United States, if not the world. Long Island is seaside, holidays, sandy toes and well-heeled ease.

Not very many resorts have this low-key, scrubbed sort of insouciance. The houses look as though they eat lots of fruit and vegetables and do yoga classes. The streets wear slightly crumpled but very clean linen. Not so much shabby as pre-faded chic. But as well as being a wealthy playground there is, of course, a local population living permanently in the Hamptons, with their stores and farms, and the artistic community that has long made it a base, being close enough to the city so as not to feel cut adrift but far enough away to offer some peace and quiet and cheap living. Living cheaply is not so easy nowadays, but in the 1950s and '60s, modest places that were not on the ocean were affordable.

My first call was to Sagaponack, near East Hampton, to visit the Madoo Conservancy. In the spring of 1966 the poet and painter Robert Dash bought an empty field in sight of the ocean, with an eighteenth-century barn, a milk house and shed. From these buildings he made a summer and winter house and two painting studios, shifting his living and working accommodation with the seasons. The garden began with a plot to grow vegetables, with paths mown through the long grass of the remainder of the ground, but gradually Dash began planting and creating spaces in an impromptu fashion, using, by his own admission, 'the wildest starts and incompletions, a long succession of blunders'.

Under the midsummer sun the garden is jumping with colour, but not so much from flowers as from paint. A bright yellow ladder leans against the shingled gable end of a building. A door of the same yellow is framed in cobalt blue, and a pillar supporting a rose with one desultory flower (the season is past) is the same vertical cobalt streak. A gazebo is lavender-mauve with a plum base, and one of the low-slung buildings has a pink door, blue window frames and bright yellow railings around its flat roof.

The garden is a slightly uneasy mixture of received good taste – such as box balls and clipped hedges, pleached trees sheltering urns, a rill and a potager – and the playful, almost perverse impetuosity that Dash admitted was the driving force behind its creation. The more Dash's whims and fancies leap out and jostle with one another, the more the garden becomes magical. The more solemn and grown-up the design and layout (and, tellingly, this tends to be the case the further you are from the studio), the less convincing it becomes. It is an artist's garden, as though the sections and pots and even groups of plants are sketches, half-finished paintings and sculptures leaning against the studio wall or set to one side to be worked on in due course.

Director Alejandro Saralegui, who has run the garden since Dash's death in 2013, told me that Dash said it had 'English bones and American flesh'. But Dash never visited England, and this is an Englishness of the bowler-hatted, Mary Poppins kind. The American flesh is much nicer and truer to itself.

The garden dances when it is at its most compressed and jumbled, in the areas directly around the barn and studio, the painted wood striking out at odds with the too-fat clipped yew and box, and the bare stems of the privet – almost a weed on Long Island – grown knobbly and gnarled like, as Dash's friend the English garden writer and designer Rosemary Verey said, 'an aged ballerina's knees'. This aged gardener's knees felt a tinge of empathy with that.

This is all completely at odds with prairie gardening or the idea of reaching out to a frontier. In fact it has the energy and irreverence and compression of the city, set in the clear light and open freedom of Long Island.

Marsh House

East Hampton, New York

I went from the Madoo Conservancy to Marsh House in Springs, owned by Edwina von Gal. Springs is both the most exclusive and the most artistic area of Long Island. Kurt Vonnegut (whose house next door to the Madoo Conservancy was the farmhouse of which Robert Dash's studio barn was once part), Jackson Pollock, Willem de Kooning, Philip Roth, Jospeh Heller, John Steinbeck – the roll call of artists and writers who have lived and worked there is long and stellar.

I knew of Edwina's work as a landscape designer and environmentalist. She is an advocate of zero chemical use and of maximum integration of wildlife and all aspects of the natural world in gardens and man-made landscapes. In the context of the conventional American garden, this is pretty radical stuff. However, the approach to Marsh House down a wooded lane gave no indication of the astonishing view that her beautiful, wooden-box-on-stilts of a house has over the Kaplan Meadows Sanctuary. The marsh, still and green like a perfectly flat meadow, is squared with drainage ditches as though lightly touched by a vast grid. The absolute blue of the water reaches across to the houses and trees of Gerard Drive, and in the hazy distance the Montauk spit of the island probes the Atlantic. An osprey's nest on a pole with three fully fledged chicks sticks out of the marsh a few hundred yards from the large deck, and to the right, perhaps half a mile away, a telescope reveals a bald eagle's eyrie with two full-sized, brown-headed young. A deer steps through the marsh and slips into the trees. These sights alone made my trip worthwhile. Garden talk is all bonus.

What Edwina is trying to show in her garden is that the natural world and gardens need not be mutually exclusive. But she is the first to admit that this is an experiment, with her 4 acres around Marsh House her laboratory. When she came here in 2004 there was a lawn in front of the house. This is now strimmed down to about a foot high – so as

to retain cover for invertebrates – once a year in spring. Otherwise, it is just left. She planted trees, but the deer promptly ate most of them. She is also planting species like sourwood (*Oxydendrum*), which come from the south, to see if they will adapt this far north as the climate changes. There are nectar-rich plants for the pollinators and everywhere neat heaps of composting brash and stacks of cut wood, creating slowly decomposing walls and shelter both for the plants within their lee and for insects and small creatures in among the wood. 'Nothing leaves the site,' Edwina says. 'Even stuff that would be considered infected or full of weed seeds I have a special pile for, because ultimately nature will disinfect it.'

Mind you, there is some concession to the incompatibility of sharing the natural world and the desire to grow vegetables and flowers, and there is a deer-proofed fenced area. Edwina accepts the compromise with a knowing smile. It is a tricky balance. A garden, by definition, is not natural, and yet she is trying to create one that is as natural as possible.

It is a very seductive experiment, and Edwina has the optimism that is characteristic of all the organic pioneers I have met. Whereas the conventional, aggressively chemical approach that has dominated agriculture and horticulture since the 1950s is based upon the assumption that nature is essentially destructive and an enemy to be overcome through the application of science, those like Edwina put their faith in the ultimately healing balance of nature. But this does depend upon a holistic approach whereby trees you have carefully planted, crops and sometimes whole species are lost on the way. It asks the gardener to surrender their islander mentality and become a willing component in a much larger natural web. I suspect that it is going to be a long, hard row to hoe before the average American is willing to apply this to their back yard.

Chanticleer

Wayne, Pennsylvania

When I said that I was going to visit American gardens, I would inevitably be told a list of ones that I simply had to visit, and one of the gardens that everyone included was Chanticleer.

Chanticleer is half an hour's drive northwest from the centre of Philadelphia, quickly moving out into the particularly leafy, villagey suburbia of Wayne. In fact when Adolph G. Rosengarten Sr bought 7 acres of land here in 1912 it was still essentially farmland. He was a scion of a wealthy Philadelphia family whose fortune was based on pharmaceuticals, in particular quinine, along with the slightly alarming combination of morphine, opium, arsenic and strychnine. The house the Rosengartens built on the land was their summer retreat until the mid-1930s, when they moved there permanently. By then the grounds had extended through the purchase of neighbouring properties, and the current garden covers 35 acres.

Adolph's son, Adolph Jr, worked at Bletchley Park in England during the war, and when he returned to the Rosengarten estate he and his wife, Janet, began to garden enthusiastically and actively. After the death of his mother in 1969 Adolph Jr took over the whole garden, although he never lived in the main house and instead used it for entertaining, centring the garden around it. In 1976 he set up the Chanticleer Foundation to 'Operate the property as a beautiful public garden, maintain the Chanticleer House as a museum, and educate amateur and professional gardeners'. To this end there are Chanticleer scholarships that send young gardeners to places like Kew and Great Dixter in the UK to broaden their education, and there is an endowment that provides the garden with an income of around $4 million a year. In 1993, three years after Adolph Jr's death, the garden was opened to the public. Since then visitors have risen to around 60,000 a year, and I was told that there is no desire or need to increase that. There seem to be no financial pressures, no drive to increase visitors, no weddings or corporate events, no café or shop to increase spending per head. Chanticleer luxuriates in a well-endowed ease that gives it the confidence to do what it pleases rather than what it feels is expected of it.

This freedom to change and experiment is what makes the garden exceptional. Almost all private gardens that are subsequently opened to the public expressly seek to preserve the garden as it was either in its heyday or at the time of the creator's death. But Chanticleer has never had that mission. Adolph Jr left no instructions as to how the garden was to be run, but the generosity of the foundation means that it can afford a high level of both maintenance and skill – and this has encouraged innovation.

Apart from Bill Thomas (and his dog Monty), who is in overall charge, there are another seven head gardeners, each of whom has autonomy over a separate part of the garden. These areas are almost independent satellite gardens within the wider estate. Each of these head gardeners is responsible not just for the maintenance of their various respective charges but also the planting and design. In principle they can do this unilaterally, although in practice Bill has a watchful eye over everything and all the gardeners discuss things with each other. Supporting this horticultural officer class is a team of assistants, interns and scholars.

The result is that different sections of the garden differ hugely from each other. It is almost like visiting the Chelsea Flower Show and going from show garden to show garden, albeit unified by huge sweeps of lawn and magnificent trees. Chanticleer thus has the great virtue of being a garden that feels alive and dynamic and a melting pot of ideas and skills. But it also has the drawback of lacking a unifying hand. The whole does not really equal the sum of its parts.

Opposite The mixture of plants allows for a range of wonderful shapes to appear.
Overleaf The Chanticleer house with its mansard roof, overlooking the flowery lawn.

It supports my long-held theory that a garden can only ever be successfully made by one or two people. Any more and it becomes a committee – and committees, famously, find their horses become camels.

Yet you could argue that this diversity, with its attendant dynamism, variety and opportunity for so many different kinds of horticultural expression, is as apt a symbol of America as you might find. Add to that the wealth, aspiration, European influence and sheer can-doery and you have the archetypal American garden. Perhaps. Inevitably, a garden of this kind ends up being a curate's egg – there are bits you like and other bits not so much. Variety and eclecticism can become incoherence.

The entrance is clever. It is a small courtyard, rich with containers, that leads through a door into the Teacup Garden, lushly exotic with bananas, gingers, bromeliads, phormiums, agaves, blazing salvias and a water feature of an overflowing cup at its centre. Go round the corner of the building and flowering hostas spread by the hundred beneath a large oak. Throughout the Philadelphia region I saw hostas growing in almost every garden, often as a bright wave of flower and never with any evidence of a single nibble by slug or snail; yet back home by far and away the most common question I am asked is how on earth one can grow hostas without them being reduced to shreds and tatters. The answer, I was told, is the absence of hosta-eating snails – although not, presumably, of snails altogether.

What were once orchards are now stands of black walnut and cherry with large flowing beds and a drive that swings round to the main house, arriving at a forecourt that is now a gravel garden raked Zen-like into concentric circles. Round the corner a terrace reveals a huge sweep of lawn flowing downhill to the Asian Woods and the Pond Garden. Tucked out of sight on the right is the Ruin Garden, where Adolph Jr's old house was razed to build a folly. The slick stonework and absence of crumbling dereliction means that the structure does not make a convincing ruin, but there are very nice things in it, such as the huge water table like that at Villa Lante, and it is a good if wildly extravagant conceit. But to complain about extravagance is to miss the point. There is a sense that they could – and would – do anything to make the garden continue its journey into being.

Hence the elevated walkway from the house to the Serpentine Garden, which curves sinuously down the steep slope around the thalictrums and coneflowers. I also loved the flowery lawn on the back terrace outside the house, with gaura, verbena, *Ammi visnaga*, fennel and sunflowers when I visited, and apparently a mass of daffodils and yellow tulips in spring. It is cut back to the ground in November, the bulbs do their stuff in spring and then the flowers, raised from seed, are planted in plugs in spring. Not so much a wildflower meadow as a tame-flower one.

In the end, Chanticleer is about plants rather than design. It is a place to dip and browse, learn, make notes, question, be inspired, be provoked and have your horticultural horizons expanded. All of which is exactly what Adolph Rosengarten Jr wanted to achieve: mission accomplished. There is a huge amount to admire – not least the professionalism and enthusiasm of the gardeners, each with their own principality within the Chanticleer kingdom – but when I visit any garden, regardless of situation or size, above all else I look for a sense of place, of unique identity, and it remained elusive. The ability of Chanticleer to change and swing and evolve dramatically is an inspiration to all gardeners. But it is also the reason why it is perhaps easier to admire than to love.

Opposite top Garden pavilion covered with *Hydrangea petiolaris*.
Opposite bottom Mown grass and stone walls elegantly mirror the curves of a small stream.
Overleaf View from the terrace by the house. One of the many images of a crowing cockerel to be found throughout the gardens at Chanticleer.

Rittenhouse Square

Philadelphia, Pennsylvania

When in 1682 William Penn took possession of the 45,000 square miles that had been granted to him by King Charles II, he determined that the new city he would build by the Delaware River would be a model of civilised, modern urban life.

He wrote: 'Let every house be placed, if the person pleases, in the middle of its place as to the breadth way of it, so that there may be ground on each side for Gardens, or Orchards, or Fields, that it may be a green Country Town, which will never be burnt and always be wholesome.' This new city was laid out in a grid with a public square at the centre of each quarter, and one of these was Rittenhouse Square, built in 1683 and known as Southwest Square until 1825, when it was renamed after the local astronomer and clockmaker David Rittenhouse. By the nineteenth century it had become a desirable address, and at the beginning of the twentieth century it was redesigned to add layers of sophistication in the shape of pools and fountains; but essentially the square and its function as a public garden in the centre of the city has remained unchanged since the end of the seventeenth century.

Our hotel in Philadelphia was just round the corner and I walked around the square a couple of times before breakfast, enjoying the shade from the tall trees even at that early hour. It was busy with people on their way to work, cutting through the square with that particular upright, focused stance that people adopt as part of their walking commute, as well as dog walkers, their bodies relaxed and pace slower, meeting other regulars and sharing doggy stories. As one who loves dogs of every kind and missed the companionship of my own on the other side of the Atlantic, there was a homeliness in this, a familiar bond to share just by being there in the square with them.

Penn's ideals still seemed present at Rittenhouse Square, not least in its relative modesty and scale. It is not a park and yet it is more than just a municipal green space. It is a garden and in many ways more personalised, more famous and much more horticulturally prestigious than some others that I was to visit in Philadelphia.

Longwood Gardens

Kennett Square, Pennsylvania

Longwood, half an hour's drive west of Philadelphia city centre, is enormous, a super-sized portion of a garden. The estate and gardens run to over 1,000 acres and have 80 full-time gardeners, plus seasonal gardeners and students, plus over 800 volunteers. It has the scale and ambition of Versailles or Hadrian's Villa – and yet its origins were relatively humble.

Pierre S. du Pont, like the Rosengartens at Chanticleer also from a wealthy Philadelphia chemical manufacturing family, bought Peirce's Park in 1906. He was in his mid-thirties and this was his first foray into anything agricultural or horticultural. But he liked trees, and as Peirce's Park was being sold on the strength of the timber to be realised by felling the magnificent trees in its 15-acre arboretum, Du Pont bought it, by his own admission, as much to prevent the felling of the trees as anything else. Changing the name to Longwood, he began to make a garden there, which from the first was on the grandest of grand scales, although the house was modest and remained relatively so for a man of his enormous wealth. However, in 1914 he added a new wing and infilled the space between the old and the new buildings with a conservatory.

The story goes that when Du Pont was eleven years old, he was walking down a street in Philadelphia and saw a wonderful conservatory. Although he longed to go inside he was restricted to gazing at it, but vowed that one day he would have a conservatory of his own. When he was nineteen he visited London and made pilgrimages to the Crystal Palace and the Palm House at Kew. He was fascinated by the workings of these giant glass palaces; and his other great interest was hydraulics. Subsequent visits to Villa d'Este, with its operatic waterworks, and Versailles fuelled this passion, which found dramatic expression at Longwood.

Clearly his first conservatory did not even begin to satisfy his needs, because in 1919 he built a neoclassical orangery that was substantially bigger than his house. Covering over half an acre and originally standing alone well away from the house, it has a kind of crazy grandeur both as a building and, inside, as a plant hall, with huge, dramatic displays. In time this orangery was added to with an exhibition hall, a music room, a ballroom and an east conservatory, so that there are now over 4 acres under glass, including lawns, landscaped waterfalls, enormous hanging baskets, tree ferns, cannas by the hundreds, strelitzias, and everywhere a kind of interior bedding like lines of showgirls swinging through the building. It has the effect of a vast floral banquet with attendants pressing more and yet more food to feast upon. There is no ambiguity about this, no coyness or false modesty: this is showtime and deliberately intended to impress and entertain. But it does not feel like a display of wealth or designed to inspire envy or even admiration for Du Pont as such. It feels as though it is a show put on for the delight of those who see it, and, this being America, the best shows are the biggest and glitziest. By all accounts the Du Pont summer parties, held in and around the conservatory in the 1920s and '30s, were the highlight of the season.

And the party still rolls on, but instead of being the most exclusive ticket in town, anyone with the $25-dollar entrance fee can come along – and more than 1.5 million people a year do. The seemingly limitless money is not just seen in the bigger, flashier aspects of Longwood. The details are all superbly done, whether in the plant labels, the way the drains are made, the lighting, the paving or the hose reels – these are things that I know as a gardener eat up money but which make a big difference if they are done well. At Longwood they are all done very well.

Walking around Longwood (and that in itself is a lengthy business) is not so much like visiting a theme park as a

Opposite Steps leading down to the Italian water garden. Note the water running down the steps.
Overleaf The fountain display overlooking the formal garden at the centre of Longwood – Louis XIV might have envied it.

funfair or festival. If the topiary is not big enough for you, then catch the 90-acre prairie-wildflower meadow; or take a stroll along the 200-yard-long Flower Garden walk, with flanking herbaceous borders set out rather stolidly in blocks of gradated colour designed by Du Pont himself as one of the first things he did when he bought the park; or visit the open-air theatre where once 1,500 guests could watch over a hundred performers, mainly dancing in a rather wafty way as was the fashion in the early 1920s. But whatever your horticultural fancy, everyone always turns to the Fountain Garden, with over 1,700 computer-controlled jets and 5 miles of piping all synchronised to a medley of rousing orchestral music. In 2017 this had a $90-million facelift to make it even bigger and more dramatic and thus, of course, even better. People love it and even in this age of computer graphics and games come for miles just to see these real-life, real-time aquatic displays.

If that leaves you overexcited and exhausted then the Italian Water Garden with its six basins arced by jets of water and a large central fountain shooting into the air, all flanked by lime trees beneath which more jets play, should soothe yet entertain your frazzled senses. This was apparently entirely engineered by Du Pont and has real charm, although the broad expanses of green paths suggest he was more interested in function than form.

The only other garden I can think of that takes such obvious pleasure in its own performance is Villa d'Este, in Tivoli, near Rome. But there is an openness and an ingenuousness at Longwood, coupled with extreme skill, that is fun. To criticise it for being a bit over the top is like criticising a carnival for being noisy or poppies or peonies for being bright. It is what it does. The scale is integral to the soul of the place and much of its attraction. Yet the bit of the garden I liked most – and I like Longwood a lot – was the parkland around the large and small lakes; and Peirce's Park, the original group of trees that prompted Du Pont to buy the place, with broad lawns broken by mature trees in the English landscape tradition. Perhaps it is because here the trees do not need the hand of man or money to be magnificent.

Previous The palm house, on a scale that rivals Kew's.
Opposite top The Italian Water Garden. All the complex hydroengineering was designed by Du Pont himself.
Opposite bottom The topiary garden with fountains behind.
Overleaf Part of the prairie meadow at Longwood.

Fallingwater

Mill Run, Pennsylvania

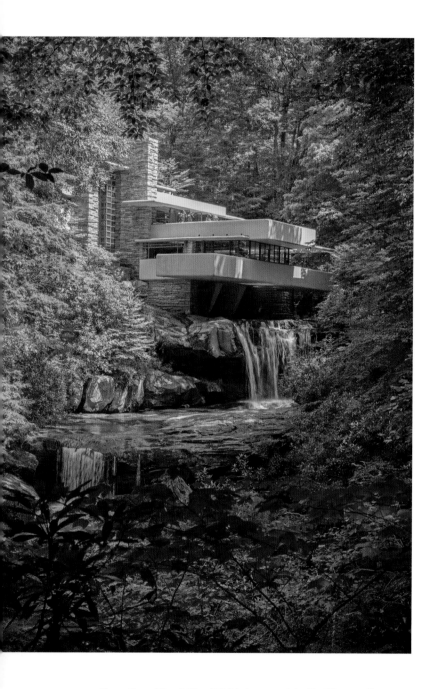

Above One of Frank Lloyd Wright's most original buildings, Fallingwater
in Mill Run, Pennsylvania, was built for Edgar J. Kaufmann between
1936 and 1939.
Opposite The house is set in dense woodland.

Kentuck Knob

Dunbar, Pennsylvania

Above and opposite Frank Lloyd Wright's Kentuck Knob (or Hagan House; 1953–56), like his Fallingwater of two decades earlier, is set in a forest. Seen here are two installations by British artist Andy Goldsworthy in the house's extensive sculpture garden.

Overleaf The house successfully merges into the landscape. The stones that compose the wall are of local rock.

Federal Twist

Stockton, New Jersey

They say that the result of most job interviews is decided by the interviewer in the first thirty seconds. Everything that follows is either challenging the decision made or else going through the motions to validate it. But the heart, or, perhaps more accurately, the gut, usually knows what it likes long before the head has even framed the question. So when I knew I loved Federal Twist garden the moment I stepped out of the car, I did not question my judgement so much as feel delighted by it. It was, from that first thirty seconds on, a treat.

The garden, near Stockton, New Jersey, was a last stop halfway on my journey from Philadelphia to New York before catching a flight back to London. If not an afterthought it was certainly a conclusion to an intense few weeks of garden visiting, and proved to be a deeply satisfying one.

Compared to the self-consciously gardened extravaganzas of Longwood and Chanticleer, Federal Twist walks a masterly line between seeming to be an easy green flow of plants and the absolute precision that is applied to every plant, every placing and every decision in order to make the whole thing seem artless. It has been carved out of the trees, with over eighty junipers taken down to create a 2-acre plot, and retains the sense of being a clearing that would be quickly reclaimed if left alone.

James Golden and his husband Phillip Saperia bought the house and plot in 2004, did some work on the house and moved in a year later, using it as a weekend home from their work in New York. James is the gardener – or, more accurately, as I was to find out, the one that is obsessed by gardens and plants. James and I sat in the garden, completely surrounded by plants towering over us. I asked him what the garden was like back then. 'There were juniper trees and almost nothing else all the way up to the house,' he said. 'There was no light, no open space. I didn't choose the place because it would be a good garden. I knew it would be very

difficult.' Having cleared away the trees he then found that the soil was heavy clay that remains saturated for much of the winter. On top of that, it was full of rocks. 'But', he said, 'I made a bargain with myself that I would find out how to make a garden here.'

He began to experiment with plants, without any clear vision for the garden other than that it would be naturalistic. But, as he pointed out, prairie or meadow planting depends on rather poor soil. His clay, although hard to work, was high in nutrients. His approach was radical, and although he makes it seem haphazard, even feckless, it was clearly based upon much thought and a deep knowledge of his plants. He did not prepare the soil in any way and did not clear the weeds or undergrowth beyond mowing it. Instead, he planted directly through it into the heavy, wet, rocky clay. Although believing it important to grow native plants where possible, the conditions meant that he chose large specimens of vigorous plants, selected for their ability to cope with stress and competition rather than provenance. Thirty *Filipendula rubra* 'Venusta' with candy-floss heads of pink flower held on stems 6 to 7 feet tall were some of the first to go in and are still going strong. The Joe-Pye-weed, *Eupatorium*, another 6-foot giant, was immediately at home. But much did not work. The first to fail were the prairie plants. 'Monarda immediately died. Echinacea immediately died.' But some grasses did well. While panicum couldn't successfully compete with the incursions of other plants into its root systems, miscanthus was a success and fought off neighbouring roots. From the first this was survival of the fittest – gardening red in tooth and claw.

Unsurprisingly, some weeds were fittest of all. Mare's tail (*Equisetum*) remains irrepressibly present and is accepted if not encouraged: 'In the spring it's beautiful because it is one of the first things to show.' James waved his arms at

Opposite James Golden cut down over eighty trees to create the garden but left a few such as this, with sinuously pruned branches.
Overleaf Different textures play an important part in the garden. The seemingly wild effect has in fact been carefully planned.

the surrounding vegetation. 'In spring none of this is here. We cut and burn while the snow is still on the ground, in late February to early March. I avoid the shrubs but the miscanthus burns cleanly, as do all other dried stems.' This is prairie management. 'I used to call this a wet prairie', James said, 'in the middle of a wood.'

This incongruity is, of course, what makes this at once both a garden and also interesting, thoughtful and dynamic. Everything about Federal Twist simultaneously challenges and breaks every rule while sinuously obeying the laws of plants and how they can grow. This takes great expertise, patience – and the willingness to fail. James said that it took about six years of experimentation before it began to feel like there was really a garden here: 'There were a lot of empty spaces, a lot of fringes that were not dealt with.' But those plants that could cope with the hostile conditions thrived and spread. Now, James says, from early summer most of his gardening activity is removing plants. Again, this takes great knowledge and a degree of courage. Editing is the hardest – and most important – horticultural skill of all. For most gardeners the temptation to allow a good thing to become too much is too hard to resist.

I suggested that the garden was driven much more by the conditions – the ecology – than James's desire to grow particular plants. In other words, the garden shapes his choices rather than vice versa. 'To me, a garden is about mystery and beauty and aesthetics and life and death,' he said. 'To call it just an ecological garden reduces it – although the ecology is so important. But there is a moral element too. The garden is good for me psychologically and spiritually, and good for the earth.' I said that all these different aspects and gifts of gardens were obvious to me and to many British gardeners but seem to be shared by few Americans. Why is that? James was hard put to answer. 'I am acutely aware that my garden is very atypical in America and would not be widely understood. But', he added, 'when we open the garden, which we do every year, half the people are locals and they seem to love it. They like the leaning feel of the plant structures, the flowers, the relaxedness. It's something new for them that a garden can do this.'

Of all the people I spoke to in hundreds of conversations right across America, James was the wisest and most gifted gardener. His knowledge and love of plants and gardens is a deep, deep seam. But as we got up from our seats he astonished me by saying, 'I forgot to mention that I hate gardening.' It was probably a well-rehearsed line but, given the extraordinarily beautiful garden he has created and the deep pleasure that it clearly gives him, an effective show-stopper. Why? I asked. 'I hate getting my hands dirty, I hate struggling to separate roots and then digging a hole. I have someone to do that for me. I place the plants, pull plants out. I'm constantly working out what I need and where to move things. I don't feel it necessary to dig or plant to be fully engaged with the garden.' I suspect that the British, and in this I include myself, fetishise the actual process of gardening too much, sometimes to the extent that the hardworking, skilful means justify the rather dull ends.

Whether he has dug every rocky hole himself or not, James has made a magical, superlative garden. Undoubtedly the limitations and difficulties of gardening on this site have helped that. They have meant that all his resources as a master plantsman and aesthete have to be bought into play, and they also make the business of editing simpler. The fact that his choice of plants has been severely limited by the conditions has made the garden better.

But it is not a simple garden. The choice and relationship of the plants, the layout with paths winding through the seemingly endless beds, the subtlety and apparent simplicity of the planting, the selection of the hard landscaping materials and the way they are used all show great sophistication and skill. It is a deeply serious garden, but there is a playful wit to it and it is entirely devoid of solemnity.

I spent one of the hottest afternoons of my life at Federal Twist when all common sense dictated that one should be indoors in an air-conditioned building. But I could not get enough of it. It is a masterpiece.

I headed back to New York and from there back home, inspired and fired by it to a greater extent than by any garden I had seen for a long time.

Above The garden has a playful character to it.
Overleaf A selection of plants thrive alongside one another, allowing a fantastic variety of shapes and colours.

JOURNEY

THREE

Phoenix

Arizona

I like the desert. It is a romantic ideal, a beautiful, stark dream drip-fed by fiction, film and the very few brief encounters I have had with it. Perhaps it is because it is so superficially un-horticultural, so different from my everyday lush green world. So flying into Phoenix, Arizona, I was as excited as a child heading for Disneyland. It did not disappoint. Huge saguaro cacti standing like sentinels in the dry stone of the hillsides; red rock pitted with caves; creosote bushes looking wind-whipped as they followed the lines of the washes down the hillsides; and, above all, that clear, hard-edged, dry sunshine.

At the end of a particularly damp and dreary northern October it was a luxury to seek shade, the sun hot but, like a racing car idling along, with just enough edge to hint at its summer ferocity, when the heat can rise above 120 degrees Fahrenheit (50ºC) and venturing outside is like opening an oven door.

Phoenix lies right at the northeastern edge of the Sonoran Desert. This is bigger than the entire United Kingdom, covering over 100,000 square miles and running down deep into Mexico, taking in a chunk of California on the way. I was told that it averages 7 inches of rainfall a year, and that falls only in two seasons, meaning months of drought every year. However, this is actually twice as much as in other parts of the desert and explains the relatively large number of trees and shrubs and the possibility of gardening.

Driving through the suburbs of Phoenix, as well as the incongruity of lawns and rose beds I saw a number of gardens that were desert-themed, with a mix of cacti, grasses, palms, mesquite and agaves artfully assembled in a setting of gravel and rocks that were not just an acknowledgement of the prevailing conditions – and therefore the horticultural sophistication to know that working with nature is smarter than trying to subdue it – but also attractive and inspiring. New housing estates on the edge of town that abutted on

unmodified scrub displayed the dramatic difference between the idea of desert, gardened and made domestic, and the reality, which inevitably has less apparent diversity and appears thinner and pared down to basic visual rations. Good gardens are always an interpretation of reality in the same way that a good portrait is more than merely an accurate likeness.

Desert Botanical Garden

The Desert Botanical Garden in Scottsdale, half an hour's drive out of central Phoenix, was founded in 1939 as a centre for the research and preservation of desert plants in the southwestern states of America. Since then it has grown and now gets over half a million visitors a year; when we got there at nine in the morning the car park was already full and the temperature was climbing into the 90s. The cacti are green silhouettes holding poses against the luminous blue of the sky. Cacti are now ubiquitous in Britain as an easy and cheap houseplant, sold by the trayful as eggcup-size plants and collected rather as we used to collect certain toys as children, to make a line on a windowsill. They have, for many people without gardens, the virtue of being the least plant-like plant they can own – the Western equivalent to Japanese *kokedama*. But I suspect that many of these cacti collectors are unaware of how majestic some species can be and how American all cacti are. They have become broadly associated with desert – wherever that desert might be – but all cacti are native to the American continents.

I have visited the Desert Garden at the Huntington Botanical Gardens in San Marino, California, but that, for its impressiveness, is a garden among gardens, like a specialised

Previous The Desert Botanical Garden in Phoenix: cacti, adobe wall and strong shadows. This could only be in Arizona or New Mexico.
Opposite Monty gives us a sense of the scale of these great saguaro cacti, which are native only to the Sonoran Desert. They grow very slowly but can reach 80 feet tall and live for hundreds of years.

wing of a large museum. It was also, the day that I was there, pouring with rain and under unbroken cloud. The Desert Botanical Garden in Phoenix is entire unto itself and is lit by desert sun. The connection with the surrounding landscape is visceral. And for all the seriousness of research and botanical complexity and biodiversity – the garden has more than 25,000 different plants from more than 4,200 taxa in more than 100 plant families – there is a stark simplicity about the place, and that makes it very easy to enjoy and admire.

I chatted to Kimberlie McCue, the director of research, who explained to me that despite the desert's vastness and the apparent abundance of cacti – and in the garden they have over 12,000 different kinds in the National Collection, massed and grouped into an intense and dramatic display of columnar, organ pipe, ball, plate, spiky and fuzzy coral-like variations – cacti as a family are the fifth most endangered organisms on the planet. The threat is threefold. The first is loss of habitat as buildings spread inexorably outwards into the desert. The second is connected to the gardens that I saw on the drive out here: the ease, despite their spines, with which cacti can be removed from their natural habitat and sold to gardeners. For example, the round barrel cacti that look like spiny pumpkins and are ubiquitous in gardens are in fact becoming very rare in the wild, simply through poaching. Finally, climate change is having an impact by subtly but critically altering the desert temperature. Katie explained to me that the Sonoran is getting hotter and drier. Cacti and all succulents are evolved to cope with drought, but they do this by restricting both growth and flowering, which in turn reduces propagation and spread of the species. More alarming is the change in temperature, which has drastic, if unexpected, consequences. 'The breaking point for cacti is when the night-time lows do not go below 90 degrees Fahrenheit [32°C]. They literally start suffocating.'

Saguaro (*Carnegiea gigantea*) are found only in the Sonoran, and the Desert Botanical Garden has over a thousand of them. They are extraordinary plants. They start from a seed the size of a poppy seed and will only reach a quarter of an inch in the first few years, taking perhaps fifty years to reach 3 feet, but they can eventually grow to 40 feet tall – with the tallest ever measured almost twice that – and live for hundreds of years. They will develop branches – or 'arms', although they are more like fat fingers clutching upwards at the sky – after fifty or so years, depending on the rainfall, and will start to flower after about thirty years. These appear in spring, opening after sunset and then closing up again in the heat of the day, and are pollinated by bees, hummingbirds and bats and become red, fleshy fruits. Saguaro expand and contract like an accordion to store water; a mature plant can hold over 1,500 gallons of water, weighing over 5 tons. A more alarming fact is that their shallow roots make them easy, despite the spines and weight, to dig up, move and replant in a garden – for which you can charge a lot of money. The result is a depredation of the natural stock that will take up to fifty years to replace. As if all this was not bad enough, the moved plant will probably die, although it will take two or three years before that becomes apparent. Everybody loses.

One final saguaro fact: there is a law in Arizona specifically prohibiting the shooting of saguaro cacti. You have been warned.

Opposite top The desert outside Phoenix. One wouldn't be surprised if John Wayne galloped past.
Opposite bottom Desert landscape with cacti that almost seem to be marching.

Palo Cristi Garden

Like me, Steve Martino loves deserts. But unlike me, Steve really, really knows deserts. Steve Martino also loves gardens, and he has spent his life combining these two passions into making gardens that use and celebrate the desert – not as a pastiche like the front gardens of Arizonian suburbia, but tapping deep into its soul to distil its essence. He has described his style as 'weeds and walls' because desert plants have for so long been regarded as weeds, and he has from the first used them with the conviction that they are not just beautiful but right and can be combined with the extreme man-made artificiality of a landscaped garden – the 'walls' – to make something that loses neither the soul of the natural planting nor the domesticity of a good garden.

Opposite Interior and exterior almost merge. Note the coloured wall outside, which sets off the cactus so beautifully.
Above Steve Martino on the terrace at Palo Cristi.

I had seen pictures of Steve's work that had a poetry and purity about them, so was delighted when it was arranged that I would meet him at the private Palo Cristi garden he had made at the edge of town, where Paradise Valley peters out into the Phoenix Mountains Preserve. It has that feel of all housing venturing into land previously untouched by man, half swagger and half the awkwardness of the gate-crasher. The desert is buried under tarmac and turf and the gardens mostly derive their style from an unholy marriage of Tuscan villa and golf course. But the curving bedrock drive to Palo Cristi, flanked by mesquite and cacti, deliberately celebrates both the harsh beauty and spirit of the surrounding landscape and opens out to reveal a handsome house, the walls on the southern side broken by tall slit windows but at the back, in the shade, almost all glass. A splash of Barragán red covers a large side wall – the owners discovered Luis Barragán's work on a trip to Mexico and apparently asked Steve to include these direct influences – and the early morning sky is already azure blue, but the plants and gravel are bleached down to greys, glowing soft greens, glaucous blues and tawny stone.

Steve is tall and laid-back with a shock of white hair and the ease of a man who has worked out what matters and pretty much gets it. This was a garden he made twenty years ago, although with some changes, and it is now mature, which is unusual for the area with its constant urge to change, improve and expand.

Ironwood trees, agave, ocotillo and cacti spread shadow patterns on the pale grey walls of the house. 'These shadows', Steve tells me, 'are more important design features than the plants themselves. You have to design with light in the desert. The light is always harsh so you soften it by playing with shadows, and that gives you movement.' Softness is an odd word to use in the face of the spines and angles of the plants and the grit and stone underfoot, but I am thinking like a northerner. Shade is the ultimate friend here, and in its embrace light and heat provide the softness you need – and all the softness you are likely to get.

Steve said that he designed his gardens from inside the house because for half the year it is far too hot to be comfortable outside. So his desert gardens are a series of tableaux to be viewed from inside, where the linear qualities of the branches and shadows play across the line dividing inside from out.

'My interest has always been in living with the desert, and that's what this garden represents. The essential thing for any garden in this part of the world is privacy and shade. A garden should be a sanctuary. I don't want to see my neighbours – in fact I don't want to see their houses – and I don't want them seeing me. So the first thing to do is screen them out.' This, compared with the all-American suburban idiom of tightly mown lawns running unscreened to the sidewalk and the openness that proclaims you to be a good and honest neighbour, is radical stuff. But Steve shrugs and smiles. 'Its very simple. In fact, all you need in the desert is trees and dirt. All my gardens have just four elements: water, tree, chair, wall. If you want to make your garden bigger then just add some more, or some, of these four.'

He is being disingenuous of course. The garden is sophisticated, meticulous and a brilliant mix of the idea of the desert sitting comfortably with the clean, bold lines of confident luxury and wealth: the long basins of water patterned by the branches of the mesquite tree, the big walls painted red and blue, the huge outdoor fireplace and the huge panes of glass revealing an ultra-stylish interior. For all his modesty, the garden has not just shambled gently into place. American money does not really do shambling. It is a highly professional, smart operation by a master designer remaining absolutely true to his inner calling – which is the desert. And the result is a stunning, inspiring garden.

Opposite The vertical strangeness of cacti creates a series of carefully positioned sculptural shapes and spaces against the backdrop of the painted walls.

California

Sunnylands

Palm Springs is less than an hour's flight west of Phoenix but, despite also being in a bone-dry, blisteringly hot plain set in the Colorado Desert, all similarities end. It is another world altogether.

We arrived after dark, but the next morning the horizon was made from the San Jacinto hills, rose-pink in the dawn sun, and down below thousands of palm trees created a green fringe all but obscuring the streets. In fact there is only one palm that is native to Southern California, the Colorado fan palm, which in the groves where there is sufficient water for it to grow is chunky and, given the right environment, statuesque. But the iconic tall palms that line the streets of Palm Springs and Los Angeles are the introduced Mexican fan palm, planted because of its association with exotic holidays, sun and pleasure. They are a marketing ploy – and one that has worked supremely well.

Set off in any direction and that green becomes almost comical as well over a hundred golf courses glisten a gleaming green as sprinklers by the thousands water the freshly reseeded fairways in readiness for the new tourist season. I have no interest in golf at all, but there is no doubt that all these tightly mown, controlled swathes of green with their inevitable palm trees are beguiling. But there may be a lot less of this golfing landscape over the coming decades as fewer and fewer young people are interested in golf and as the existing golfers get too old to swing a club in anger. This will change Palm Springs dramatically because all that manicured green depends entirely on people paying a great deal for the pleasure of playing golf on a verdant course in the middle of a desert.

Nevertheless, my first destination was a house with a golf course built around it – in fact, at that time, only the second private golf course to be built in the entire country. This was Sunnylands, built by Walter and Leonore Annenberg in the early 1960s. Even the bits that are not golf course – the huge lawns, the groves of trees, the long drive that sweeps towards the house – look like one. Take the golf out of the course and what you have is slightly monotonous, over-pampered parkland with large stretches of tightly mown grass. The fact that cacti grow around the fringes of the house and the surrounding scenery is of bare mountains adds a magic to the incongruity, but for all its size the garden element is minimal.

But Sunnylands is important and was very influential. Walter Annenberg was heir to a publishing company that made him enormously rich through magazines such as *Seventeen* and *TV Guide*, the latter of which was selling a billion copies a year at its peak, as well as television stations and newspapers including the *Philadelphia Inquirer*. His wife, Leonore, was raised by her uncle Harry Cohn, who was head of Columbia Pictures, which gave her a lifelong connection to California and Hollywood. The couple became prolific collectors of art – in particular Impressionist and Post-Impressionist paintings – and major philanthropists, ultimately giving hundreds of millions of dollars to cultural, educational and medical institutions as well as donating their billion-dollar art collection to the Metropolitan Museum of Art in New York. From the 1950s they began to spend winters in Palm Springs, and in 1963 they decided to build their own estate. So they bought over 900 acres of land in what was then empty desert on the edge of town and transformed it into their own golf course wrapped around a large single-storey house that, with its central pink pyramid roof, looks like a cross between a chapel and a motel but which was, by all accounts, large, luxurious and filled with treasures.

Opposite Early morning on the Sunnylands estate, where the Annenbergs tamed the desert and made the first golf course (a private one) in Palm Springs.
Overleaf Pool reflecting the various cacti, notably the barrel ones. This part of Sunnylands was created by the Annenberg Trust.

The result is the antithesis of everything that Steve Martino has spent his life creating, with all the creosote bushes, rock and sand bulldozed to make way for 180 acres of mown turf and 6,000 trees, mostly eucalypts, oaks, olives, tamarisks, oleander and carob. The story goes that when President Eisenhower came to play golf he noticed that, unusually for Palm Springs, there were no palm trees, so two were dutifully added and are still known as the Eisenhower Palms. On top of these there were thirteen lakes (and to ensure the water supply, as well as that for watering the grass, Walter simply bought the local water company), a swimming pool and a rose garden. Sunnylands even acquired, in 2001, its own 50-acre private cemetery, where the Annenbergs are both interred. It has also to be said that there is now a concerted effort to cut back on the amount of water used to keep the grass green. Sixty acres have been deturfed and are either bare sand or mulched or 'pigmented' green, which adds a twist to 'greening the desert'.

This very private fantasy in the desert, just a hop from LA, was secure, luxurious and discreet and as well as a retreat for the Annenbergs became a prize invitation for a mixture of film stars, musicians, sportsmen, politicians, dignitaries and royalty. Walter Annenberg was a friend of presidents Nixon and Reagan and ambassador to the Court of St James's in London between 1969 and 1974, and his connections and friendship with the British royal family meant that when Queen Elizabeth and Prince Philip made their visit to California in 1983 she visited Sunnylands, as, in due course, did Prince Charles.

Walter Annenberg sold his media empire to Rupert Murdoch in 1988 for $3.8 billion and then spent the rest of his life giving a large chunk of that money away, particularly to educational institutions. He died in 2002, and Leonore followed him seven years later. They left Sunnylands, reduced now to half its maximum size, as part of the Annenberg Foundation, with the house and golf course as a centre of international diplomacy – a kind of safe house where high-level diplomatic talks can be held in a completely relaxed, private atmosphere – as well as the right, in perpetuity, of any president of the United States to come and use the golf course.

In 2012 the gardens were opened to the public as the Sunnylands Center and Gardens, and now around 100,000 people visit every year. There is a new 9-acre cacti and succulent garden based upon the Impressionist collection of the Annenbergs, with barrel cacti in rhythmic rows under the shade of palo verde trees like spiky clipped box balls. They make a fine set of tableaux, although the Impressionist connection is subliminal at best. There is a big round lawn where children are encouraged to play, and every effort is made to include as wide a selection of the community as possible in sharing all that the centre has to offer. It is a far cry from the exclusiveness of the Annenbergs' heyday.

Pass through the pink boundary wall of Sunnylands and on the other side of the road is white desert, dotted with creosote bushes and the mountains on the horizon. Sixty years ago this was regarded as barren waste, and Sunnylands, with its hundreds of acres of healthy green grass and trees, the face of aspirational civilisation. Now the roles have become more complex, more delicate. While there is still a certain air of reverence at Sunnylands – for money, philanthropy, power, even golf – it has become a fascinating relict of a world that has moved on, and the parched subtlety of the desert scrub seems both a reproach and something closer to a sustainable future.

Opposite top A typical (or ideal) view in Palm Springs, showing the green grass with the mountains as backdrop.
Opposite bottom Overlooking one of the many ponds at Sunnylands, with trees on the far side and mountains beyond.

Rees Roberts House

Just down the road from Sunnylands – choosing a route along one of an unlikely trinity of Frank Sinatra, Bob Hope or Gerald Ford Drives – is an older, much smaller house, not with its own golf course but built right on the edge of one so that the fairway is only kept at bay by a tightly clipped pyracantha cloud hedge. This belongs to the designer and artist Lucien Rees Roberts and his architect husband Steven Harris. The house was built in 1957 in the Desert Modern style, and they have lovingly restored it. It is a cool, predominantly glass box with white walls and deep projecting roofs held by slim white columns around, of course, a pool.

The planting is wonderful, all cacti, agaves, grasses and bamboos, and seems to emanate from inside the house and sprawl out into the garden. This is because wherever you look, either inside out or outside in, you can see through the huge windows to more garden on the other side of the building and the rooms become another garden space. This effect is deliberately played upon by planting along covered walkways and in the building itself. The whole plot is relatively small but seems much bigger as a result. It also means that the approach to creating a border or balanced mix of plants has to work just as well from the back, side and front. There is no behind the scenes. Everything is open – a kind of stylish and clever variant of the lawn running down to the road that declares you open to scrutiny.

I asked Lucien if living right on the edge of a golf course was not a little too open and public. He reassured me that the members of this course are all elderly and move slowly, and they hardly play anyway. Golf, it seems, is dying a slow death in Palm Springs. However, if I were him I might be worried about what might replace the open greenness of the links, because unless it becomes a private park it will almost certainly become more housing.

By ten in the morning it had become very hot – too hot to sit in the sun, and this was late October. Stepping into the cool of the air-conditioned house was a joy. I could see that one of the reasons a house like this works so well with its garden is down to air conditioning. It means that you can be comfortably cool indoors while still enjoying the light and seeing your garden. But to achieve this, the garden is shut off behind a glass screen – air conditioning, after all, only works when all the windows are shut. You cannot smell the heat, let alone the plants. You cannot feel the breeze or the sun. The garden becomes at best a lovely series of scenes at a remove from the household. It ceases to be the main event and becomes a kind of embellishment or garnish to domestic life, without visceral engagement.

Opposite Sprinklers play on the (public, but little frequented) golf course, seen from the swimming pool of the Rees Roberts House.

Kaufmann House

To the northwest of Palm Springs, right on the edge of town, far from any golf course, is a relatively modest house and garden that was, and in many ways still is, a potent icon. This is a house designed by the architect Richard Neutra for the department store owner Edgar J. Kaufmann to spend his winters. (Kaufmann's summer home was the seminal Fallingwater in Pennsylvania, designed by Frank Lloyd Wright, so he can lay claim to having commissioned two of the most iconic twentieth-century American buildings.) It was built in 1947 and is still the epitome of Desert Modernism.

The date is important. I recall my mother talking about the winter of 1947 as being the lowest point of her life. In the aftermath of war, Britain was exhausted physically, financially and emotionally. Rationing was drastic – far harder than at any stage during the war itself. Then came the snow and bitter cold of one of the worst winters ever recorded in the UK. Electricity and water were often cut off and fuel hard to come by. My mother told me how she had to walk 5 miles in the snow with my newly born sister to fetch coal, which she then pushed back in the pram with my sister. George Orwell famously wrote of burning his son's wooden toys for fuel. Not only was there snow and constant biting cold but for the whole of February 1947 many parts of the UK barely saw the sun. It was bleak and desperately harsh.

So this house by the Austrian-born Neutra with its cool, confident American lines, the swimming pool dominating the garden and the mountains behind, all under a blazing blue sky, was a dream beyond the wildest European imagination. If this is not the archetypal icon of the American Dream – a little too sun-kissed and easy for that – it certainly exemplifies California Dreamin'. It has the same impact as a Hockney painting; a place where not just sunshine and leisure are endlessly available but also freedom from the sexual and social constraints of hidebound European life.

Air conditioning was not installed when the house was built, and it shows in the way that interior and exterior merge and flow in an almost unbroken manner. The steps of the pool run across almost the entire width of the garden and start from the house, so there is no break, no season of 'going outside' to play or relax. It is a seamless line of pleasure. Like Sunnylands, the house was originally set in the desert, but unlike Sunnylands was open both to be seen and to the view – and that openness was part of the brave new Californian modern world it represented. It is now surrounded by other houses and has a high hedge to protect it from the coach-loads of tourists who come to try and catch a glimpse of it – not, I suspect, for its iconic architectural status so much as for the fact that it once belonged to the singer Barry Manilow.

Opposite Slats of light slip through one of the walls of the Kaufmann House.
Overleaf The swimming pool, known from an iconic photograph taken by Slim Aarons in 1970.
Pages 172–73 The carefully planted garden at the rear of the house uses the desert and its vegetation rather than trying to escape it.

Bob Hope House

Palm Springs, California

Dawnridge

Los Angeles is an incoherent city. It sprawls and leaches and amasses itself into quarters without ever really arriving or leaving anywhere. Yet, as the Southern Californian landscape designer Scott Shrader said to me, 'it has the best weather in the world', and since the gold rush years of the mid-nineteenth century the combination of sun, opportunity and possible wealth and fame has made it a magnet that still draws millions. The fact that most gold panners barely found enough gold to pay for board and lodging, and that today most would-be stars end up waiting tables, does not deter people. They still keep coming.

I visited a couple of private gardens within a mile or so of each other in Beverly Hills that showed two faces of the same strange LA coin. Dawnridge belonged to Tony and Elizabeth Duquette and epitomises the world of fantasy held together just long enough for the camera to roll or the party to last. It is a garden cobbled together from bits and pieces and is all smoke and mirrors – and yet it works. It is fabulous and fun; and it is truly glamorous, although only just. It is a conjuring trick that you almost work out before the denouement but find yourself applauding nevertheless.

The house was built in 1949, so it is almost the same age as the Kaufmann House in Palm Springs, but in every possible way it is a world apart. It is in a side street on what was a deep canyon occupied by scrub and eucalypts. The exterior is modest enough, save for the giant sun above the door, but you enter into a cluttered doll's house of a building, impossibly crammed with furniture, paintings, sculptures and what are best described as artworks because they fall

outside any easy categorisation. But absolutely nothing in either the house or garden fits into any easy categorisation, and that is both its key and its joy.

Tony Duquette had worked as a designer of jewellery, costumes, interiors and, above all, stage sets when he and his wife, who was a painter, moved into the house. At the time it was a tiny 30-by-30-foot box, but it nevertheless quickly became the scene of famous Hollywood parties attended by Ginger Rogers, Mary Pickford, Greta Garbo, Gloria Swanson and Aldous Huxley, among others. Marlon Brando rented the house in 1952 during the filming of *Julius Caesar*. It was never the Duquettes' only house – they lived in Paris and San Francisco and had a ranch in Malibu – but it was always a constant, and, above all, a party house.

The garden really came into being rather later, when the house next door burnt down in 1973 and Tony Duquette bought the plot to extend his garden. It is now a wild melange of Indonesian, classical, Indian and European objects and assemblies all layered upon each other. There is no attempt to hide the temporary nature – not to say tackiness – of the materials as long as the overall effect is reached. So Duquette made buildings that have a touch of Thai Buddhist stupa, a hint of Hindu temple and a smidgeon of Shinto shrine, all constructed from trellis, recycled doors, disco mirrors and fibreglass. There is a treehouse with a domed roof taken from a film set and with walls made from Second World War landing strips. There are pillars made from recycled tin cans sitting on top of ancient Islamic brass columns, unconcealed concrete block walls, old gateposts and fencing material with hinges roughly nailed to hold elaborately carved gates that are then painted and adorned and assembled to create what looks like an elaborate set for a party – which is exactly what it was.

Everything was grist to Duquette's creative mill. He travelled widely, buying whatever caught his fancy, and also

Pages 174–79 I decided to visit Bob Hope's house, drawn by how its extraordinary placement on a hillside overlooking the Palm Springs valley would photograph. It was designed in the late 1960s by John Lautner. **Opposite** Mrs Hutton Wilkinson in the garden at Dawnridge. **Overleaf** Some of the results of Tony Duquette's compulsive shopping on his travels.

recycled pieces from film sets or parties he had put on in his studio and his Malibu ranch. It is said that he was completely happy to cut, glue or paint antiques or to make a centrepiece from a papier-mâché prop from a film set balanced upon an ancient classical carving. The show was the thing above all else.

The planting, exotic, exuberant, almost entirely green, ties everything together and takes all these stage oddities and weaves them into a garden. And because the plants are living and growing they have a dynamism and future that transforms the static stage sets into something that also has a future – long after the party is over. There are dozens of palms crammed into every corner; bananas; scores of spider plants dripping from an eccentric medley of containers; crassulas and other succulents (all apparently moved from Duquette's ranch at Malibu); and far too many abalone shells crammed with plants. Duquette's motto was 'More is more', and the garden is an object lesson of the adage that if you do something with enough confidence and panache you will probably get away with it. Not that there was any sense of bluff. I am sure that Duquette was playing with plants in exactly the same way that he played with all the other materials – inventing, amassing, assembling, all to reach the effect that he wanted at that moment. The garden has that essential ingredient missing from so many gardens of the great and the good, which is playfulness. Combine that with real talent and you have something special.

After Tony's death in 1999 his business partner and inheritor, Hutton Wilkinson, became guardian of the house and garden. Despite having had to sell much of the valuable antique furniture to pay estate duties, he has kept it much as Tony would have wanted it, and inside the house has used his and Elizabeth's work exclusively. Wilkinson also added considerably to the garden. Although many others in the street had filled in their bits of the canyon in order to put in the inevitable swimming pools and tennis courts, the Duquettes had left their section untouched. So after a large tree fell, Wilkinson made a completely new part of the garden down in the canyon, with a waterfall running into a stream on which floats a Vietnamese wedding boat moored

Previous After Duquette died, his business partner Hutton Wilkinson continued to develop the garden in Duquette's spirit. At any moment you expect Ava Gardner to emerge from this Thai- and Islamic-inspired confection.

Opposite A stone dog adds to the 'sauce'.

to a platform that leads out from an arched pavilion with ornate Indian carved screens painted scarlet and turquoise. Telegraph poles topped with sunbursts of thick steel wire mimic palm trees. A sleekly modern building rises above the cascade and the foliage, not intrusive but like just another outfit in this fancy-dress garden. The light filters down through the trees, catching glinting slithers of huge koi in the water, and although it honours the spirit of Duquette it adds an uncluttered dimension and scope in a way that the upper storey of the garden does not. But both are charming and it all feels at home in this strange city.

Sheats-Goldstein House

A short hop from Dawnridge as the crow flies, but a grinding half-hour in LA traffic, is another extraordinary house and garden, equally fantastical but with a radically different character. Whereas the Duquettes' house was an unremarkable building transformed by remarkable embellishment, James Goldstein's house was extraordinary from conception. Designed and built by the architect John Lautner for the Sheats family in 1961, it is angular, dramatic and, even now, strikingly modern. After having various owners throughout the 1960s, the house was bought in 1972 by the businessman James Goldstein – avowedly to give his beloved Afghan hound more space than his existing apartment.

When I visited it, the house, for all its extravagance and architectural drama, looked as though only notionally occupied. Every surface was bare save for the odd strategic magazine or arch floral arrangement, the lines remorselessly clean and uncluttered, every finish crisp and sharp. The main embellishment were hundreds of framed pictures of Mr Goldstein posing with startlingly glamorous models.

I met Mr Goldstein at the house while a swirl of caterers, modishly dressed men, severe women in black and extravagantly tall blonde models all scurried around preparing the launch of a costume jewellery collection. For once, two of my otherwise disparate worlds made an unexpected collision (I spent the 1980s as a costume jeweller in London and worked very closely with the company in question.) Goldstein is an octogenarian with a shock of white hair and mahogany tan and, clad in running shorts and shoes and a tight T-shirt,

gave the impression he was about to set off jogging the streets rather than host a glitzy event. We stood at the sharp angle of his bedroom – one of the few private spaces not taken over by said jewellery company – and he pressed a button that resulted in the huge plate-glass windows sliding back so we jutted 50 feet out over the lushly planted slopes.

Now we have to set the record straight here. We were divided by more than a large continent and an ocean. I am a middle-aged, middle-class English man of conventional and rather dull upbringing. My domestic life, away from books, is all children, dogs, plants and muddy fields. My own house is an amalgam of different architectural periods but averages four hundred years old. To say the least, Mr Goldstein and I were an unlikely couple.

He introduced himself with a hoarse 'Whad'ya want?' 'I'd like to talk about your garden,' I said. 'No one ever wants to talk about my garden.' He made it sound like an accusation. I assured him that I very much did, and it turned out so did he. He is a serious and passionate gardener and the extraordinary jungle he has created is his baby – and obviously not one that he gets asked to share very often. When he bought the property he set about working with Lautner repairing, remodelling and 'perfecting' the house. This process seems to be continuing, fifteen years after Lautner's death, with building work in evidence, making, it seems, a new swimming pool and library.

Goldstein told me that wherever he goes in the world – and he is a fanatical follower of fashion, attending shows all over the world – he invariably visits the local botanical garden. Exotic jungle plants are his thing, and this is the only area where he and Lautner clashed. 'Lautner wanted the hillside to be more or less bare with a few pines. But I wanted tropicals,' he said. So tropicals he got – and brilliantly planted and managed they are. Steep cantilevered steps in cast concrete run down the hillside through groves of bamboos, palms, bananas, daturas, ficus, bromeliads, clivias, monstera and others I guessed at. Occasionally the vegetation clears to loom out across Culver City and downtown LA before the plants swallow you up again. Halfway down is a James Turrell skyspace, which unfortunately I could not see as it was firmly locked. I have visited the Turrell sky garden in Skibbereen in County Cork and the skyspace in the Keilder Forest in Northumberland and found them profoundly moving and

inspirational. To have your own private one in your back garden is like having a Picasso hanging in the kitchen.

'I started out just landscaping around the house,' Goldstein told me, 'but once I started I just kept expanding.' I asked if he had a budget. 'No. Nor for the house. Whatever it takes.' It has clearly taken a lot, but then he clearly has a lot and it is equally clearly a deep passion. I scanned the bookshelves and found row upon row of books on tropical plants.

Although flamboyant, dramatic and a major statement – it now covers a large hillside – there is something a little lonely about this garden, because clearly not many of the willowy models or pinch-faced fashionistas all in black would ever ask about his 'tropicals'. Yet Goldstein is evidently deeply serious about them. In any event the house and garden are entrusted as a gift to the Los Angeles County Museum of Art as a permanent legacy of Lautner's house and James Goldstein's garden.

Scott Shrader House

I had the chance to visit the garden designer Scott Shrader in his tiny garden in West Hollywood. It is enclosed by high hedges and, despite the size, divided into three rooms, including an outdoor kitchen and dining space in which to eat his homemade pizzas and drink a glass or two of Californian wine in the benign heat of an LA evening.

Scott is hugely successful in Southern California, creating gardens for the rich and famous that are designed for what is advertised as 'outdoor living', which is clearly a brand of graceful and luxurious lifestyle. I asked Scott if his clients showed any interest in gardening – as opposed to having a beautiful garden. He shook his head. 'Nope.' Why not? I asked. His answer surprised me. 'Because they are too busy.' Are they too busy for the gym, I asked him, too busy for the mindfulness session, the spinning class, the golf game, the bike ride? He laughed. 'No. They do all have time for at least some of those things.'

Previous At the Sheats-Goldstein House, overlooking Los Angeles – very much a 1960s feel. Many airports use this type of roof.
Opposite top An example of interior and exterior becoming practically indistinguishable at the Sheats-Goldstein House.
Opposite bottom The tropical planting comes right up to the glass walls of the house.

This says a great deal about America's attitude to gardens. The very successful, living here in LA's climate, want a lovely garden and want Scott's skill and urbanity to create it, but they also want cheap Mexican labour to tend it, using the appalling leaf blowers whose engines rip through the residential streets by the tens of thousands. They no more want to tend their garden than they want to wash up the meals they eat. Actual gardening is disconnected from the lovely outdoor living garden. It seems that gardening has yet to be seen as creative or fun, or even as good exercise and healthy for mind and body – just the lowly means to the end of maintaining a lovely garden.

Odyssey Charter School

But the next day my cynicism was tempered by a visit to a school in Altadena. The Odyssey Charter School has converted a large section of its playing fields into a plot with raised beds for vegetables and plenty of fruit trees and bushes, including oranges, lemons, apricots, pomegranates, tangerines, apples and pears. There is a greenhouse, a tool shed and a table for the kids to eat at.

This garden and the tending of it is an obligatory part of the curriculum for the school's five- to eleven-years-olds and then voluntary for twelve- to fourteen-year-olds. I joined a class of sixth graders, all eleven years old, as they were planting up vegetable beds that they had prepared with seedlings they had raised. They were extraordinarily bright and engaged with what they were doing at both a horticultural and culinary level, as well as with the environmental connections that this involved. On the door of the tool shed was painted in large multicoloured letters a quote from the poet and farmer Wendell Berry: 'To Cherish what remains of the Earth and to foster its renewal is our only legitimate hope of survival.'

After a very happy hour or so in their company I left with a sense that this rising generation had a much clearer and more engaged relationship with the earth, both at a hands-on, immediate level and on the broader planetary scale, than most of their adult peers – including politicians. They were learning to cherish it.

Lotusland

I like going back to gardens I have visited before, and I was on my way back to Lotusland in Santa Barbara, a couple of hours' drive north of Los Angeles. The first time round is a process of discovery and absorption of visual, practical and emotional information. So when you return there is room for all that information to become a relationship of sorts.

Stopping off in Ventura, I drank a coffee outside in the sun opposite the Ventura Center for Spiritual Living. The ocean was visible at the end of the street and the coffee was reverently prepared by a girl with a mesh of tattoos that ran seamlessly from her fingertips and disappeared under her T-shirt. A notice on the wall told me that the centre could offer me classes in being 'Wholly Abundant' or in 'Priceless Pricing' or that I could perhaps join a drumming circle. On a lovely autumnal morning, California was exceeding all expectations.

And Lotusland lived up to all my memories. My previous visit was twelve years earlier, which in the life of a garden is enough for radical change. In fact there had been no dramatic transformations, but enough to be interesting; the place is so odd, so extreme, so very eccentric that any change that diminished that would be a disaster. The estate stretches to over 30 acres in the foothills of Montecito, to the east of the city of Santa Barbara, and the modern

Opposite The cypress avenue at Lotusland. One could be in Tuscany were it not for the palm trees at the end and the un-Italian mountains beyond.

garden was created between 1941 and 1984 by Madame Ganna Walska. The Gavit family, from New York, owned the property from 1916 to 1938 and the main house was built for them in 1919, although Madame Walska always lived in the original servants' annexe and used the main house only for entertaining.

She seems to have been an extraordinary woman. She was born Hanna Puacz in 1887 in Brest-Litovsk, Belarus, became an opera singer despite reputedly having not much of a voice, and took the stage name of Madame Ganna Walska. She married six times and, like a Tudor widow, steadily accumulated great wealth in the process. By the time she came to California her sixth husband, Theos Bernard, a devotee of yoga and Tibetan Buddhism, persuaded her to buy the estate on the grounds that it would be an ideal place for a monastery for Tibetan monks. However, despite renaming it from the existing Cuesta Linda to Tibetland, the monks never came. The husband soon went – she divorced him in 1946, after which he remarried and was subsequently murdered in Pakistan in 1947 – and she never remarried. Madame Walska changed the name again, to Lotusland, and devoted the rest of her life to the creation of the garden.

It was hardly a retreat. If not actually much good as a singer, Walska was very successful as a star, and Lotusland became the scene for a succession of Hollywood parties. She was a performer and a woman of great wealth who liked to spend with extravagant largesse. And she was a very serious collector and gardener. The last time I visited, I met her niece Hanjya, who was bought up by Madame Walska at Lotusland, and she told me that her aunt never planted in ones or twos: 'If she wanted something she had to have two hundred.' She also said that no one was ever allowed to prune anything without Madame's supervision. On this visit I was told, discreetly, that she was not a fantastically good gardener – someone always had to come behind her and clear up and make good after her efforts – but she was undeniably enthusiastic.

This enthusiasm means that the garden is, for America, unusually personal and grounded in hands-on gardening.

This part of Southern California has about 17 inches of rain a year, mostly in winter, and although they have had terrible fires, it is never too blisteringly hot in summer and never very cold in winter. This means that a huge range of plants can be grown outside. And Madame Walska was prepared to go to great lengths to expand this range. When she wished to create a new cactus garden towards the end of her life she sold $1 million worth of jewellery to pay for it. She also took a shine to the dracaenas that she saw in the local front gardens, so she would go around in her chauffeur-driven car, see a specimen that she liked and send the chauffeur in to offer a price for it, and then send round her team to dig it up and bring it back to Lotusland. Before long she had accumulated a thicket of them, their succulent branches forming a canopy that still grows magnificently in front of the main entrance, while the neighbourhood languished noticeably dracaena-less.

In time she accumulated collections of rare and endangered botanical species, including important collections of cacti and cycads. But the garden is quite hard to take seriously. Across the huge lawn fringed by monster agaves, where Madame assembled the Hollywood rich and famous for her parties, is a formal section behind a vast Monterey cypress. A rose garden with two large flanking beds filled with roses – with, on my visit, the yellow Julia Childs in flower – leads via a Mughal pool and rill down to a clock the size of a roundabout that is decorated with signs of the zodiac and keeps perfect time. Around it is a menagerie of topiary figures, camels, dolphins, seahorses, bears, lions and dinosaurs all gambolling in a kind of mad roundelay. The Blue Garden is an interweaving of glaucous foliage with agaves, Chusan palm, *Festuca glauca*, Mexican blue

Opposite top and bottom Cacti and palm trees explode like green fireworks.
Overleaf Cacti rise above a wall at the end of the olive avenue.

palm, blue Atlas cedar and Chilean palm meshing together in subtle shades of blue and grey. Chunks of smoky blue obsidian, made from the clinker of a nearby glass factory, act as edging 'stones'. There is an Abalone Pool, so called because it is edged with abalone shells, surrounded by a large collection of aloes; and an 'insectary' (an area filled with pollen-rich flowers), the cycad collection, a clivia walk, a bromeliad garden, a fern garden, a Japanese garden – it is exhausting to record, and much too exhausting to visit all in one go. However, the opportunities to visit are limited by local prurience. When Madame Walska died in 1984 the estate wished to open the garden to the public, both to share it and to raise money to maintain it, but it took over eight years and sixty hearings to finally get permission because local residents did not want the traffic. As it is, the permission came with the imposition of a maximum number of only 15,000 visitors a year. I am certain you could add a zero to that figure without any trouble, and anyone within 100 miles should go along and see it before the other 14,999 use up the quota.

Above The topiary is as eccentric and eclectic as the rest of the garden.
Opposite top The Abalone Pool is planted with a large collection of agaves.
Opposite bottom Like a tight bouquet, different cacti, palms and non-tropical trees vie for attention.

The Redwoods

In a strange way, redwoods have featured across my life. From the age of seven I went to a boarding school in Berkshire that was only about 20 miles from my Hampshire home, but whereas the soil there was chalk and with its specific flora, the school in Crowthorne was on acidic sand and dominated by plants that could never grow at home, such as pines, rhododendrons, heathers and camellias. To this day they seem alien to me.

There was also a long, straight stretch of road flanked by an avenue of giant redwoods – known then as *Wellingtonia gigantea*, after the Duke of Wellington, which was the name they were first given when introduced to Britain in 1853, although the name was quickly changed to the modern *Sequoiadendron giganteum*. One day my father happened to mention that, despite being so huge, they have a very thick bark that is so soft you can punch it. He then proceeded to stop the car, go over to the nearest tree, remove and carefully fold his jacket and give it a series of hard body blows. He had been an army heavyweight boxing champion, and nearly sixty years on I can still see him, pummelling the enormous tree as though it were a punch bag before coming back to the car and driving on as though this were a completely normal part of any journey.

Many years later I bought a house in the heart of the Herefordshire countryside that had a long drive with a line of giant redwoods on one side. They were planted too close together – few in the late nineteenth century, when there was a craze for planting these American introductions, had any idea of what size they could attain – but were magnificent, if completely at odds with the surrounding landscape. I had to sell that house and the garden to pay business debts, which broke my heart, and my abiding memory of leaving is of bumping down the pitted driveway past that line of thick-barked trees with all my possessions in a horsebox.

But now I was heading up the west coast to the Henry Cowell Redwoods State Park to fulfil a long-held ambition of seeing redwoods growing in their natural environment. These were not the redwoods of Wellingtonia Avenue but *Sequoia sempervirens*, the coastal redwood, which were actually introduced to Britain a decade earlier than the Wellingtonia, in 1843. It is only found in a narrow strip about 50 miles wide along the Californian coast because it depends upon sea mist for a significant proportion of its moisture. Not only do droplets collect on the foliage and drip down to the ground, but the trees have fungi living inside their leaves that draw moisture in. This means that they have adapted to grow in an area that will not receive any rain for months on end in the summer.

While the giant redwoods are exceptionally huge in girth, it is the height of the the coastal redwoods that sets them apart from any other tree, and some of the oldest are huge. I am not sure what I expected – size, certainly, but as individual, monstrous specimens standing alone or at least apart from each other. However it is a completely immersive experience. I had not imagined how they actually grow, which is in closely set stands of trunks sometimes just feet apart and all shooting absolutely straight up beyond sight. You never see the top of a single tree. The biggest in the park is 275 feet tall and 1,500 years old (although they get much bigger even than that; there is one 379 feet tall a little further up the coast that is the tallest living organism on the planet). You crane and strain and wonder, but there is simply not room to stand back and take a measure of them.

I had not expected the cool, green stillness. A redwood forest is a quiet place. There are hardly any birds, and the mass of the trees and the 'duff' – as my guide, park ranger Steven Elmore, called the fallen twigs and foliage – absorbed

Opposite No camera can convey the height and grandeur of these trees. Monty gives some feel of their size.

and muffled most sounds. Steven told me that there are about 48,000 acres of the natural redwood forest left, which sounds a lot but is a tiny fraction of what was once over 2 million acres of these trees: 95 per cent have been cut down over the past 150 years. This devastation was based upon superficial practicality. The wood is immensely strong, straight, insect-resistant and very fire-resistant, and barely rots. In other words, it made perfect building material, and logging for their timber still goes on. After the Second World War, however, the realisation that this was a form of environmental vandalism slowly took hold and parks were established and bought up where logging could not occur. Coastal redwoods are also one of the very few evergreens that will coppice, which means that they will regrow from the roots, so there is now quite a lot of secondary growth from trees that were felled a hundred years ago or more – although those will have been thousands of years old, and these are babies. But they grow very fast initially – up to 200 feet in the first hundred years, reaching for the light – before slowing right down.

One of the features of these redwood forests is that there is so little else growing – or indeed living – among the trees. This is partly because they cast such a deep shade, but also because their leaf litter acts as a blanketing, extremely acidic mulch, making it hard for seeds to reach the soil to germinate; and even if they do, seedlings will struggle to reach the light. This does not affect the redwoods themselves because they rarely propagate from seed, with 98 per cent of all new growth coming from the roots. It means that some of the original trees, over a thousand years old, may well be regrowth from even older, fallen trees – which in

turn may have regrown themselves. The roots could be tens of thousands of years old. Despite their age the roots are shallow and seem to live in family groups so that a cluster of trees will not compete for light, whereas other trees from another group will be shaded out. The roots also support and interlock with each other, guying the trees to the ground, so they are very wind-resistant.

Ravens honked overhead but there was little other birdsong or calls. Coastal redwood bark is extremely tannic, so there are very few insects and consequently very few insect-eating birds or bats. Their thick bark – which my father right-hooked all those years ago – protects them from fire, and the tannins are also a fire retardant. As well as that, the trees create a microclimate that is some 10 degrees Fahrenheit cooler inside the forest than outside, so in very hot weather they lose less moisture. In all, they create their own ecosystem that serves them incredibly well but which is hostile to most other living things. Fires do sweep through these forests, though; and Steve reckons that each mature tree endures a blaze about every twenty to thirty years, so the older ones will have survived dozens and may even have their core wood burnt out, but the cambium layer beneath the bark survives and feeds the tree higher up, beyond the reach of the flames.

One is told not to meet your heroes, but these trees have figured as part of my private mythology since I was a little boy. Having seen the real thing I admire them more than ever. The insignificance that they expose in our little lives is curiously empowering. We use the word 'awesome' too readily, but these trees inspire profound and enriching awe.

Opposite Like the foot of some mastodon: the base of one of the redwoods.

Windcliff Garden

Indianola, Washington

Leaving the sun of California and Arizona, knowing I was returning to the British winter, was a wrench. But first we went to Seattle, which although meant fishing out jerseys and waterproofs, also meant having the chance to see some final interesting gardens before returning home.

We took a ferry across Puget Sound to Bainbridge Island on a grey, pearly morning. Commuters were muffled, bobble-hatted and hunched against the dawn chill. The desert seemed a long way away. We drove past wooden houses, maples and stands of cedars, thujas and pines to the northern tip of the island, where a modest bridge links Bainbridge Island north to the Kitsap Peninsula that convolutes itself around the sound opposite Seattle and leads to Windcliff, the garden of Daniel Hinkley and his partner, the architect Robert Jones. When I mentioned to people that I planned to go to Seattle I was repeatedly told that I had to visit Windcliff. This has as much to do with Hinkley's renown as a plantsman, author and lecturer as the fame of the garden, which is only occasionally open to the public for charity events.

Hinkley's fame centres on his achievements as a plant hunter, which has involved collecting specimens from over twenty countries, with a third of his year spent on expeditions. Many of his finds are raised in the Heronswood nursery and garden, a mile or two north of Windcliff, which he owned and ran for twenty years before selling it in 2000, returning as a consultant a few years ago when it was bought by the S'Klallam tribe. When Hinckley and Jones bought Windcliff in 2000, Jones designed the house while Hinkley planned the garden. This was an empty 5-acre plot, an exposed, more or less treeless, sun-baked, wind-blasted bluff overlooking Puget Sound with a view south to the snow-capped Mount Rainer rising above the horizon. The garden is now mature and filled with plants of huge and unexpected diversity. It is loose and flowing, without any mown grass or obvious structure other than the narrow paths that wind through it and the pools with water running down from the house. In this it superficially appears similar to a prairie garden, but that does not bear any inspection. The essence of a prairie garden is that it takes on its own flow and life, with various plants becoming more successful and dominant and others finding their own niche; it is gardened with a light hand and with the overriding premise that it should be largely left to do its own lovely thing. Windcliff is much more controlled than that. The plantsman's delight in variety and provenance means that there is little repeat planting, although many variations of themes. There are hundreds of different plants from many different continents that would otherwise never grow together but which here survive and enhance each other as a result of the gardener's skill and constant attention. Plants from New Zealand, Chile, South Africa, Provence or northern Australia all easily jostle and cohabit. It is controlled and and highly managed – albeit with the expert's deftness of touch.

As well as the plants – such as grasses, shrubs, trees and palms – and a line of yellow Tibetan prayer flags there are huge concave rocks positioned to catch water and light and provide structure. 'My father and grandfather were dairy farmers in Michigan and spent their entire life getting rocks off their land, so my father would certainly roll in his grave if he knew how much trouble and money I spent bringing rocks onto my land!' As well as looking superb, the rocks allow Dan to grow plants that need better drainage than even his sandy soil can offer in this very wet part of America.

'We thought Windcliff was a very quaint, English-sounding name,' Dan told me, 'but after the first winter, when we found ourselves harvesting kelp off the roof of the house, we realised just why it was called that!' In the warm October sun, winter storms seem a world away. But then so does England – a sea eagle drifts past the cliff face and loons call in the background. Hummingbirds flirt with the flowers

Opposite A stream runs down from the house through large rocks, all of which were hand-selected and brought to the garden.

scrambling up the side of the house. Nothing remotely English or quaint about these.

This winter exposure has meant that Dan has learned to fine-tune his planting techniques to give everything a fighting chance. He tries to raise everything possible from seed – 90 per cent of the existing garden – so plants start here as young and adapted as possible, as well as allowing him to grow in quantity and for the happenstance of hybridisation. He always plants small to allow plants to grow and adapt and become tough. He initially planted at a generous spacing, which meant that while the garden took a little longer to look good, each plant was given the chance to develop a strong root system. Dan has found that the wind dries the crowns of plants, which in many cases is enough to stop them rotting in winter – so exposure is a key to their survival.

Dan Hinkley is a plantsman and botanist to his last cell, and as with all plantsmen his garden is there to display and house his collection of plants as much as the plants serve to create the garden. 'In many ways this garden is my laboratory and my library,' he says. 'It is a reference collection of those plants that I have been able to collect in the wild.' This does not belittle the garden. It is beautiful and would still be so if you did not know the name or provenance of a single plant, but to Dan the attraction of a plant is inextricably bound with its story. I asked him if he felt the urge to make another garden, to have another big creative enterprise. 'No,' he said. 'This is where I am.' I know that sense of unity and identity when the place where garden ends and gardener begins becomes blurred. It is a profound sense of arrival.

Above and opposite Although the planting at Windcliff appears to be loose and very natural, in fact it is meticulously planned. Over 90 per cent of the plants were raised from seeds collected by Dan Hinkley himself.
Overleaf Windcliff has the feel of a garden by the sea. The water beyond is the Puget Sound.

Amazon Spheres

Seattle, Washington

Right in the centre of downtown Seattle, three huge domes sit squatly among the skyscrapers looking like overlapping dark bubbles or toadstools emerging from the ground. From the outside there is something sinister – or perhaps just excitingly futuristic, depending on your take on these things – about their appearance. I think they fit both bills. But they are also rather beautiful.

The Spheres were built in 2016–18 by the Amazon corporation for their employees, of whom there are over 53,000 based in Seattle. The idea is that the interiors of these intersecting domes provide precious and all too rare contact with nature and thus enhance the quality of employees' lives – and therefore the quality of their work. Everybody wins. The interior is like a cross between a palm house and the vast atrium of a particularly well-heeled bank. Painted welded steel hoops, triangles and girders have a structural swagger that Decimus Burton would have been proud of. The air feels fresh and there is a slight scent of rain as a huge living wall four storeys high and containing over two hundred different species of plant is gently doused by computer-controlled sprinklers. Everything is, of course, computer controlled, from the humidity and temperature to the light levels. Planters spill out little jungles of their own, and walkways take you up into the canopy of a 50-foot tall, 20-ton rusty fig (*Ficus rubiginosa*) that was craned in through the roof. Employees must apply to use the building – with a maximum of eight hundred at any one time – where they can hold meetings, drink coffee and eat doughnuts or lie out on chaise-longues, laptops (of course) on their chests, looking very busy.

It is all astonishingly well done both technically and aesthetically. There is a sense that no expense and no trouble have been spared. But it is a strange building. So much money – they would not tell me how much it cost, but certainly millions and probably tens of them – for a building that exists ostensibly to give employees the opportunity to be 'in nature'. Yet the nature that is created is exotic and it is, in every sense, a bubble. In the hills barely half a mile away are wonderful woods and gardens and the seashore with eagles, and dolphins and whales in the sound. It is as though 'nature' has become divorced from everyday life and can only be truly experienced in these spheres as virtual reality. However, I suspect that if there is a problem to this then it is mine, and as much as anything generational. We live in a world where authenticity is what you perceive and relate to in a direct way, be it in the woods, on a screen, computer-generated or crafted by hand. The plants within the spheres are every bit as real and authentic as those growing in nearby gardens – and if this stimulates a latent interest in plants and the natural world at large, then it has succeeded as well as any walk in the woods ever could.

The conception and execution of the Amazon Spheres is staggeringly good and the horticulture truly impressive. It is as powerful a symbol as any of that American frontier spirit based upon the unbounded optimism that you can achieve anything, make anything, be anything in this country if you want it badly enough and are prepared to work hard enough.

Opposite Inside the Amazon Spheres in downtown Seattle. The interior is on four levels, with plants rising from the ground to the very top.

Right The Amazon Spheres viewed from outside.

Bloedel Reserve

Bainbridge Island, Washington

I crossed back from the city to Bainbridge Island to visit Bloedel Reserve, the final garden on this journey. Bloedel Reserve is a 150-acre estate of gardens, ponds, meadows and wildlife habitats created by Prentice and Virginia Bloedel between 1951 and 1996, when Prentice Bloedel died. His wife predeceased him in 1989 and the reserve was first opened to the public in 1988, the year before her death. It now has 64,000 visitors a year from all over the world.

Prentice Bloedel's father, Julian, had established one of the largest logging companies in the world and owned vast tracts of forest in the Pacific Northwest. They cut down millions of trees. But from the start, Bloedel Reserve was intended as a celebration of living trees rather than of lumber. Although nominally still head of the company, Prentice retired in 1951 and devoted most of his time to the establishment of the reserve. Initially it was little more than logged-out marshland. But the Bloedels planted and allowed regeneration, and in the Washington climate of high rainfall and warm summers it all grew very fast. They pursued a policy of minimum interference, allowing trees to fall and slowly decay and the cycle of vegetation and regeneration to take its own time and course.

The California garden designer Thomas Church was hired to reshape the garden around the house, creating terraces, lawns and a pool with a superb view out over the sound, and various gardens were made through the years, including a Japanese garden and pavilion where the swimming pool once was; the largest moss garden in America; a large Reflection Pool; and lawns and acres of woods.

The Japanese garden is in two parts, either side of a guest house built as a hybrid between the longhouses of the indigenous peoples of the Northwest Coast, a swishly modern house with huge plate-glass windows and a traditional Japanese building – and the result is surprisingly successful. Directly outside the building is a dry garden with stones and raked gravel swirling around them, made on the site of the old swimming pool. The paving that once bounded the pool has been laid in chequerboard fashion with grass and moss squares, providing a loose patchwork effect. It works well because it is also a hybrid, taking influences and using them rather than slavishly reproducing a true Japanese *karesansui*, or dry landscape garden, in every precise detail. As I was looking at it, musing over the intense care that the Japanese give to placing stones in a dry garden, a visitor crunched across the raked gravel, climbed up onto one of the stones in the traditional triad to take a selfie with an outstretched arm and full-toothed smile, and inspected it proudly as she ambled back across the gravel. I did not know whether to be shocked and outraged by her irreverence or applaud the Zen-like spontaneity.

Down below the guest house is a Stroll Garden designed by the Japanese American gardener Fujitaro Kubota. It is fine but, unlike the dry garden, slips into parody; nice, but a rather pointless exercise in this context. The Bloedels were greatly influenced by Japanese approaches to nature and the visitor is encouraged to regard the garden as a process through which you experience the natural world, rather than a series of horticultural tableaux or rooms. While it is all carefully and beautifully managed and maintained by a large team of gardeners, natural decay and growth is encouraged and its beauty valued as highly as carefully raised plants. A great deal of work and effort goes into keeping the place looking as untouched as possible.

This is a fine line to tread, and there are areas where either horticulture has too heavy a hand or design tries too hard. But by and large it works, and works well, and in places it is breathtakingly beautiful.

Opposite Autumn colours at the Bloedel Reserve.
Overleaf Almost all the trees in the garden were planted by the Bloedels, despite the family having once owned the largest logging firm in America.

The moss garden was created by removing almost all the undergrowth from that section of wood, leaving just huckleberries and the tall cedars, and was originally planted with 250,000 plugs of Irish moss. However, most of these these promptly died. But the Bloedels resisted replacing them and found that gradually they were replaced by indigenous mosses, until now there are over sixty different indigenous moss species, jostling for space and ascendancy and covering the woodland floor in an undulating, velvety carpet that creeps over and into the fallen trees and 'snags' (stumps) and around and under the ferns. Despite the care that went into its creation, unlike a Japanese moss garden there is no sense of this being tended in minute detail, but of the forest slowly reverting back to its natural, prelapsarian state.

It is, however, part of a progression along the moss-lined path that arrives at an unclipped yew hedge and its visible red-barked frame of trunks and stems. An opening turns out to be into an enclosure that has a long black rectangular pool, surrounded by a frame of mown grass to the water's edge and the yew hedge, now tightly clipped, and behind that a wall of giant green trees on all four sides arriving at the same sky that is reflected in the pool. It is a stunning piece of garden design in its own right and, when taken as part of the progress through the mossy wood, worth crossing the continent to see. It made a fitting end to an extraordinary, albeit limited, tour of America via its gardens, and there is a horticultural treasure trove to dip into right across the nation.

Any visitor who travels at all widely in this extraordinary country is repeatedly staggered by its beauty and size. But America is yet to form a broad-based garden culture. Perhaps this is all part of the very American gulf whereby a reverence for landscape precludes the same degree of engagement or wonder for the back yard. I can think of no other country where such a high degree of urban sophistication exists along with such a variety of unspoilt natural landscape. It seems that for many Americans, to go out and hike in this wilderness fulfills the need to cultivate and nurture a garden.

Gardening is a form of cultivating one's own inner space. Much of the reward comes from the connection between the gardener's spiritual and aesthetic sense of self and the outward show of the garden. Each enriches the other, and to cultivate a garden is to cultivate your soul. But as James Golden said at Federal Twist – a garden that grows ever better in my mind – America has been built on the notion of constant expansion. As a nation it has yet to learn to do more with less. America is yet to celebrate the ordinary.

But it will. While many are still seduced by the extraordinary and the extreme, pushing out as though there were no boundaries as to what man can do to nature, there is a growing sense among a younger generation that this earth needs our careful and urgent care if we are not to despoil it forever. It needs looking after. And the best place to begin that, to make that care part of the fabric of your life, is in a garden.

Opposite top A weeping willow looks like a sculpture of a very old man crawling.
Opposite bottom The beautifully simple Reflection Pool.
Overleaf Over sixty different kinds of native mosses spread over the roots of the trees.

Index

Page references in *italics* indicate pages with images.

Opposite There is a nice story attached to these palm trees at Sunnylands: soon after the Annenbergs had moved in, Dwight D. Eisenhower paid a visit. While admiring the transformation of the desert and the green of the lawns for the golf course, he pointed out that there were no palm trees, whereupon the two shown here were planted.

Acknowledgements

It has, as always, been a great pleasure working on this book with Monty Don. It's the fourth book on which we have collaborated and the pleasure – for me, at any rate – hasn't diminished.

I would like to thank all the owners of the gardens featured in the book. I owe special thanks to Sir Peter Crane, President of the Oak Spring Garden Foundation, who made a great difference to my visit there; and likewise to Gregory Callimanopulos, for his kindness in allowing me to photograph Medway. Also to Lord and Lady Palumbo for allowing me to photograph their house, Kentuck Knob, for helping arrange Fallingwater and for their exceptional hospitality while I photographed these places.

My thanks to Tim Gleason, who arranged for me to photograph the Bob Hope House in Palm Springs as well as the Sheats-Goldstein House in Los Angeles.

Likewise my thanks to Peter Dawson at Grade Design, who has made the final layout under quite difficult circumstances, which required extra patience.

Anna Godfrey, my editor at Prestel, has faced a difficult task in accommodating the various demands of this book, as has Andrew Hansen, and I much appreciate their contribution.

Thanks also to my assistant, Raffaella Matrone, and to Sinéad Bligh, my previous assistant.

As ever, huge thanks to Brent Wallace for his invaluable help in the selection and editing of the photographs.

My friend Joe Holtzman not only helped in selecting the photographs and creating a guide to the layout but contributed hugely in creating the spirit of the book, which would not be the same without him.

Finally, a big thank you to my wife, Alexandra, who has helped throughout this project.

DERRY MOORE

I would especially like to thank all the owners, gardeners and guides of these gardens, who gave us so much of their time and hospitality and showed such warmth and enthusiasm in doing so.

My assistant Polly James in the UK and Miranda Soto in Los Angeles ensured that everything worked like clockwork, and between them they made life very easy.

Mike and Steve Robinson and Robert Leveritt were the best of colleagues and travelling companions and set professional standards that were an inspiration.

My collaborator, agent and friend Alexandra Henderson overcame every and any obstacle from conception to the very end and did so with unflagging energy, enthusiasm and good humour.

At Prestel, Aimee Selby edited and improved my text with tact and intelligence and Anna Godfrey oversaw the enterprise with charm and great forbearance. To both I am extremely grateful.

It was, as ever, both a privilege and life-enhancing good fun to work and travel with Derry.

But my greatest thanks go to Sarah, for supporting me through thick and thin.

MONTY DON

© Prestel Verlag, Munich · London · New York
A member of Verlagsgruppe Random House GmbH
Neumarkter Strasse 28 · 81673 Munich

© for the text by Monty Don, 2020
© for the photographs and captions by Derry Moore, 2020

Front cover: Lotusland, California
Back cover: Monty in Phoenix, Arizona

A CIP catalogue record for this book is available from the British Library.

Editorial direction: Anna Godfrey
Copyediting: Aimee Selby
Design: Peter Dawson, Ronja Ronning, gradedesign.com
Production: Friederike Schirge and Andrea Cobré
Separations: Repro Ludwig, Zell am See, Austria
Printing and binding: DZS Grafik, d.o.o., Ljubljana
Paper: Profisilk

Verlagsgruppe Random house FSC® N001967

Printed in Slovenia
ISBN 978-3-7913-8675-1
www.prestel.com